# Moments of Truth

# Moments of Truth

## Jan Carlzon

**HARPER**

NEW YORK · LONDON · TORONTO · SYDNEY

# HARPER

A hardcover edition of this book was originally published in 1987 by Ballinger Publishing Company. It is here reprinted by arrangement with Ballinger Publishing Company.

First PERENNIAL LIBRARY edition published 1989.

Library of Congress Cataloging-in-Publication Data

Carlzon, Jan.
  Moments of truth.

  "Perennial Library."

  Reprint, with new introd. Originally published:
Cambridge, Mass.: Ballinger Pub. Co., c1987.
  1. Scandinavian Airlines System—Management.
  2. Aeronautics, Commercial—Sweden—management.
  3. Airlines—Sweden—Management.  I. Title.
HE9860.S28C37  1989      387.7'065'485      88-45644
ISBN 0-06-091580-3

22 23 24 25 LSC 80 79

# CONTENTS

# FOREWORD

Imagine that there's a loose panel in the passenger compartment of the New York to Los Angeles airplane. The panel has a sharp, protruding edge that has torn the stockings of a passenger who reports it to the nearest flight attendant. The flight attendant can't repair the panel herself because she doesn't have the proper tools. She needs help. The only thing she knows to do is file a report that will end up in an office somewhere. But the office contains only a telephone and intercom; no tools. Meanwhile, our flight attendant has delegated the problem upward in the company. To her way of thinking, she has done her job. Late that afternoon, the report will be sent to a corresponding level of another department. A half-hour later, it is placed on the desk of someone in the technical department. The technician isn't sure whether or not he can fix the problem. But he needn't worry. By now the plane is flying at 31,000 feet over Dubuque. The technician scribbles a directive on the now dog-eared form: "Repair when possible." And it will be repaired—10 pairs of torn stockings later.

Jan Carlzon's answer to this? Get rid of the horizontal barriers to communication. Turn middle managers, "hired to make sure instructions are followed," away from the role of administrator and into leaders and facilitators for the frontline people who serve the customer and market.

After all, the first 15-second encounter between a passenger and the frontline people, from ticket agent to flight attendant, sets the tone of the entire company in the mind of the customer. This is what Carlzon calls the "moment of truth."

Who is Carlzon? In late summer 1986, *Business Week* described how Sweden "became Europe's powerhouse. . . . Ten years ago it was the 'sickest of sick men.' Now it's the envy of the continent." No one better exemplifies what *Business Week* calls "the aggressive, fast-moving management style that has made winners out of many Swedish companies" than SAS's Carlzon.

At age 36, in 1978, he took over Linjeflyg, Sweden's domestic airline, thus becoming the world's youngest airline president. Following a People Express-like strategy, he slashed fares, filled seats, and achieved exceptional success in record time. His reward was the presidency of SAS in 1981. After 17 consecutive profitable years, the airline had racked up $30 million in losses in 1979 and 1980.

Employees ruefully awaited his arrival. More cost cutting and fare slashing was expected. Instead, Carlzon created "EuroClass," first-class service at coach rates, as part of his single-minded focus on the business traveler in an effort to become "the best airline for the frequent business traveler" in Europe.

In short order, punctuality became the best in Europe; remarkably, SAS returned to profitability in just a year, while the rest of the international airlines tallied a record $2 billion collective loss. By 1984, SAS had been voted *Air Transport World*'s "Airline of the Year."

To be sure, Carlzon's story in *Moments of Truth* is the saga of an extraordinary turnaround in the volatile airline business, but its general applicability knows no bounds. He argues, correctly I believe, that we are at an "historic crossroad." Our traditional (Western) competitive advantages have been badly eroded.

We are entering, Carlzon contends, a customer- and market-driven era. Wiser consumers and new competitors, from air transport to autos to semiconductors to financial services, are turning up the heat on traditional businesses. To deal with this market-led discontinuity, we must revolutionize our organizations. Specifically, says Carlzon, the "customer-oriented company is organized for change." It will simply not survive with detached, administrative, top-down leadership.

This book is chock-a-block full of instructive stories and practical advice, describing Carlzon's activities at Vingresor (the package vacation subsidiary of SAS, where he assumed his first presidency at age 32), Linjeflyg, and SAS in particular. He began at Vingresor as an order giver, not a listener—neither to his people nor to his customers—and made every mistake in the book. By the time he got to Linjeflyg four years later he had learned many lessons; in fact, he began his second stint as top dog by calling the entire company together in a hangar and asking for help—a far cry from his barking out commands just 48 months before.

At SAS, he arrived at a time of crisis. He concluded that service and the frontline people who delivered were the success levers. He shifted focus from the plane as physical asset to the customer. He stunned the technocrats by mothballing his big Airbuses and flagship 747s, keeping instead the older, less efficient DC-9 fleet that provided the flexibility necessary to best serve the cherished business traveler.

Carlzon and his newly energized team boldly mounted 147 service improvement projects, at a cost of about $50 million, despite the still-flowing red ink. He also cut to the bone all costs that didn't serve the airline's single-minded goal. For instance, a 40-person centralized market survey unit was disbanded—market data collection was to be done locally; that is, closer to the ultimate customer.

Carlzon charged the frontline people with "provid[ing] the service that they had wanted to provide all along." He spiffed up uniforms, transferred autonomy to the field, and encouraged people not to take "no" for an answer. For instance, in support of the business traveler, separate Euro-Class check-in was desired. All the experts pooh-poohed the idea. The regulators would never permit it, given Sweden's pronounced egalitarian philosophy. Ignoring its own experts, SAS plunged ahead, and the request was approved.

Empowerment of frontline people to get on with it is one ingredient. Leadership is another. Carlzon's leadership formula (proven by him in practice) is unconventional to say the least. He slams professional management as it has evolved. He honors intuition, emotion, and showmanship. Analytic thinkers "are often disastrous decision-makers and implementers," he asserts. The analysis-bound professional manager dreams up new alternatives in order to avoid making decisions. At Carlzon's SAS, "analysis is always directed toward the overall business strategy, not toward the individual elements of that strategy."

The new leaders' tools are a clear, concise vision and consummate communication skills—with soul. There is nothing soft and squishy about it. Carlzon calls the new executive (and himself by implication) an "enlightened dictator."

Loyalty to the vision, not the details of execution, is a must—or else. People shine only if demands are sky high, he believes. Part and parcel is rigorous, honest measurement. Tough, visible goals, aimed at serving the customer and measured so as to engender unit versus unit competition, spur the process onward.

Enlightening as all this is, the best is yet to come. SAS leapt hurdle after hurdle, far ahead of schedule, between 1981 and 1984. Then the energy began to wane. After about a year's soul searching, with much dissipated momentum in its wake, Carlzon launched "the second wave." It is an ambitious program aimed at a major improvement in efficiency in order to proactively prepare for impending European airline deregulation.

The goal is worthy, but the process of achieving it profound—providing exceptional insights that go a long way toward explaining why most U.S. turnaround efforts have run aground. Carlzon acknowledges having "hot-wired" the system at the outset to breathe new life into the frontline people. They were SAS's heroes. Nothing was to get in the way of their providing superior service. Should a middle manager demur, the first line was vigorously encouraged to go around him or her, directly to the top.

To be sure, the process worked. But it does not, says Carlzon, form the base for sustained vitality. Middle management must be ignited and redirected toward serving the market, too. The initial short-circuiting of middle management, Carlzon admits, did not contain "viable alternatives to their old role as rule interpreters." "We had let our middle managers down," he now says.

The second wave's answer to achieving unheard-of efficiency is not—once more—an issue of improving physical assets. It is a people issue, through and through. The "distribution of roles is radically different"; the pyramid, that is, must be flattened once and for all.

Will Carlzon achieve a second miracle? We don't know yet. But his prescription is on the mark, I feel. From bank to boilermaker, the typical U.S. firm's response to the economic revolution engulfing us has been hardware first, people and organization second. The wisest heads, usually ignored, have warned that this was a perilous course. Automation will not save a poorly laid out factory with demotivated workers. A bigger computer will not save a bank in the volatile world of financial services, where bold new products are being launched daily.

As Carlzon suggests, our organizations must literally be turned upside down. We must learn to welcome change rather than fight it, to encourage risk-taking rather than snuff it out, to empower rather than demotivate our first-line people, and to focus outwardly on the fast-changing market rather than inwardly on Byzantine bureaucratic maneuvers. To this list Carlzon adds his brilliant analysis of the middle manager, so often ignored in the transition program—and so often the eventual dragging force that slows down the best-intended programs. He also underscores the tough-minded role of the new visionary leader: vision and trust, yes; but with loyalty, rigorous demands, and customer-focused measures.

One would hope that Carlzon's colleagues—and all managers—in the U.S. airline industry will read this book. Uncompetitive service—despite attractive prices—eventually humbled recent highflier, People Express. Merger digestion problems and frantic responses to deregulation have resulted in a generally intolerable level of service for the American business traveler—and big losses for many of the flailing airlines to boot. Only American Airlines—which has, alone among the majors, been the sole carrier to eschew sizeable acquisitions—is in the pink of health; its service still tops most charts, and its strategic use of information is plowing new ground for all service industries. With Delta as a second exception, the frequent flying customer has been left out in the greedy rush to expand at a rate that even minimum service cannot match. One suspects that many of the huge dollar losses and much pain could have been avoided if Carlzon's methodology had been applied by his American counterparts.

*Moments of Truth* is a book for U.S. airline executives and U.S. bankers, for U.S. textile makers and machine tool purveyors. It is a marvelous contribution to our urgent effort to fundamentally redefine our organizations for the brave new world that is upon us. It provides examples, suggestions, and, above all, a new philosophy—from someone who has been on the firing line and achieved brilliant turnaround successes in record time.

—*Tom Peters*

Everyone needs to know and feel that he is needed.

Everyone wants to be treated as an individual.

Giving someone the freedom to take responsibility releases resources that would otherwise remain concealed.

An individual without information cannot take responsibility; an individual who is given information cannot help but take responsibility.

—*Jan Carlzon*

# Moments of Truth

# A MOMENT OF TRUTH

Rudy Peterson was an American businessman staying at the Grand Hotel in Stockholm. One day he left the hotel and headed for Arlanda Airport, north of Stockholm, to accompany a colleague on a Scandinavian Airlines flight to Copenhagen. The trip was only for the day, but it was important.

When he arrived at the airport, he realized he'd left his ticket back at the hotel. He had set it down on the bureau to don his overcoat and had forgotten to pick it up.

Everyone knows you can't board an airplane without a ticket, so Rudy Peterson had already resigned himself to missing the flight and his business meeting in Copenhagen. But when he explained his dilemma to the ticket agent, he got a pleasant surprise.

"Don't worry, Mr. Peterson," she said with a smile. "Here's your boarding card. I'll insert a temporary ticket in here. If you just tell me your room number at the Grand Hotel and your destination in Copenhagen, I'll take care of the rest."

While Rudy and his colleague waited in the passenger lounge, the ticket agent dialed the hotel. A bellhop checked the room and found the ticket—exactly where Mr. Peterson had said it would be. The ticket agent then sent an SAS limo to retrieve it from the hotel and bring it directly to her. As it happened, they moved so quickly that the ticket arrived before the Copenhagen flight departed. No one was more surprised than Rudy Peterson when the flight attendant approached him and said calmly, "Mr. Peterson? Here's your ticket."

What would have happened at a more traditional airline? Most airline manuals are clear: "No ticket, no flight." At best, the ticket agent would have informed her supervisor of the problem, but Rudy Peterson almost certainly would have missed his flight. Instead, because of the way SAS handled his situation, he was both impressed and on time for his meeting.

I'm very proud of the Rudy Peterson story because it reflects what we have been able to achieve at SAS. We have reoriented ourselves to become a customer-driven company—a company that recognizes that its only true assets are satisfied customers, all of whom expect to be treated as individuals and who won't select us as their airline unless we do just that.

As SAS we used to think of ourselves as the sum total of our aircraft, our maintenance bases, our offices, and our administrative procedures. But if you ask our customers about SAS, they won't tell you about our planes or our offices or the way we finance our capital investments. Instead, they'll talk about their experiences with the people at SAS. SAS is not a collection of material assets but the quality of the contact between an individual customer and the SAS employees who serve the customer directly (or, as we refer to them, our "front line").

Last year, each of our 10 million customers came in contact with approximately five SAS employees, and this contact lasted an average of 15 seconds each time. Thus, SAS is "created" 50 million times a year, 15 seconds at a time. These 50 million "moments of truth" are the moments that ultimately determine whether SAS will succeed or fail as a company. They are the moments when we must prove to our customers that SAS is their best alternative.

If we are truly dedicated to orienting our company toward each customer's individual needs, then we cannot rely on rule books and instructions from distant corporate offices. We have to place responsibility for ideas, decisions, and actions with the people who *are* SAS during those 15 seconds: ticket agents, flight attendants, baggage handlers, and all the other frontline employees. If they have to go up the organizational chain of command for a decision on an individual problem, then those 15 golden seconds will elapse without a response, and we will have lost an opportunity to earn a loyal customer.

This approach may seem to turn the traditional corporation upside down. It does, and I believe that is necessary. The traditional corporate structure resembles a layered pyramid with a pointed top, several intermediate levels, and a base connected with the market. At the top of the company sit the chief executive and a number of highly qualified vice presidents—well-educated, skilled specialists in finance, production, exports, and sales. The task of this top management group is to control operations by making all the decisions necessary to run the company.

The sheer number of decisions that must be made

keeps them occupied with the decision-making process, necessitating that intermediaries convey these decisions throughout the company. So a large corps of people in middle management converts top management's decisions into instructions, rules, policies, and orders for the workers at the bottom level to follow. Although these people are called "middle management," they are actually not managers at all if by "manager" we mean someone who makes his own decisions within a sphere of responsibility. In reality, they are just messengers who relay decisions made higher up in the corporate pyramid.

At the bottom of the pyramid are the foot-soldiers, which include both blue- and white-collar workers. These are the people who have daily contact with the customers and who know the most about the company's frontline operations. Ironically, however, they are typically powerless to respond to the individual situations that constantly arise.

Yet the business environment upon which this hierarchical corporate structure was based has changed. In today's global economy, Western industrialized nations are no longer protected by their traditional competitive advantages, which once allowed Europeans and North Americans to produce and sell their goods exclusively in local markets. Cheap raw materials, cheap labor, and advanced technological developments are now found in the Third World. Today cows are slaughtered in Texas and the hides are sent to Argentina for tanning and then on to Korea to be made into baseball gloves. Finally, the gloves come full circle and are shipped back to Texas where they are sold to local sporting goods shops.

Increasingly unable to compete from a production-oriented advantage, the Western economies are being transformed into "service" economies. We are at an historic crossroad where the age of customer orientation has arrived, even for businesses that have never before viewed themselves as service businesses.

A Swedish manufacturer of welding equipment, for example, had long monopolized the European market with its high-quality products. Suddenly the company discovered that it had lost nearly half of its market. Apparently a European competitor was selling less sophisticated equipment for half the price—and satisfying both the customers' needs and budgets. The Swedish company, by setting its own production-oriented agenda, had priced itself right out of the market. In today's world, the point of departure must be the customer—not the production tools or technology itself—and this means that companies must organize themselves differently to survive.

In a customer-driven company, the distribution of roles is radically different. The organization is decentralized, with responsibility delegated to those who until now have comprised the order-obeying bottom level of the pyramid. The traditional, hierarchical corporate structure, in other words, is beginning to give way to a flattened, more horizontal, structure. This is particularly true in service businesses that begin not with the product but with the customer.

In order to become a customer-oriented company, extensive changes will be required on the part of frontline employees. Yet, the initiative for those changes must originate in the executive suite. It is up to the top executive to become a true leader, devoted to creating an environment in which employees can accept and execute their responsibilities with confidence and finesse. He must communicate with his employees, imparting the company's vision and listening to what they need to make that vision a reality. To succeed he can no longer be an isolated and autocratic decision-maker. Instead, he must be a visionary, a strategist, an informer, a teacher, and an inspirer.

To middle managers he must delegate responsibility for analyzing problems, managing resources and, most importantly, supporting the needs of the frontline employees. In fact, there is tremendous opportunity to be found in a "new breed" of highly capable and well-educated young people who are eager to accept the challenges of responsible management. We must give this new breed an active role in modern business, charging them with real responsibility and showing them respect and trust.

To frontline employees the leader must pass along the authority to respond to the needs and problems of individual customers. Like the agent who arranged to pick up Rudy Peterson's forgotten ticket, frontline employees must be trained properly so they become empowered to respond to customers' unique needs with speed and courtesy.

By reapportioning responsibility in this way, companies can maximize their "moments of truth." They will multiply their happy, satisfied customers and, thereby, secure an important competitive advantage.

Many of you are probably thinking, Why does an executive from a small country in Northern Europe think he can lecture Americans on how to run their companies? The answer, I think, is that the business changes I am describing here have been forced on us more rapidly in Scandinavia. An accelerated process of social and economic leveling has forced Scandinavian leaders to rethink and adjust both ourselves and our organizations. I believe that the way we have responded in Scandinavia in general and at SAS in particular provides an example from which business leaders in the United States and other industrialized countries can benefit.

# 2

# THE VINGRESOR AND LINJEFLYG TURNAROUNDS

## Vingresor

In June 1974, at the age of 32, I sat down behind the desk in the president's office of Vingresor, a subsidiary of the Scandinavian Airlines System that assembles and sells vacation package tours. I'd been selected president after only six years of working life. I had authority over 1400 employees, many of them roughly the same age as I. My qualifications were no better than anyone else's, and there was no obvious reason for making me president. I was afraid—afraid that I wouldn't be accepted and afraid that I would fail.

So I began acting the way I thought a boss should act. I straightened my tie and summoned my staff. One after another they trooped into my office, and I issued firm instructions about what was to be done:

"Change that timetable!"

"Make a deal with that hotel!"

At every meeting, no matter what the situation, I'd deliver my edicts:

"Now I want this!"

"Now I've done this!"

"I think this!"

What I was going through was, no doubt, what most of us experience the first time we find ourselves in the spotlight. I began behaving differently because I was acting out the role I believed I'd been given. I assumed that everyone at Vingresor expected me to be able to do everything better than they could, and that I should make all the decisions.

So I tried to live up to these expectations. People began hearing my voice more and more often. I had the solutions to everyone's problems—as if I instantly had acquired wisdom along with the presidency. I made countless decisions with very little knowledge, experience, or information.

Around the office I became known as "Ego Boy." The nickname was borrowed from a famous racehorse of the time, but it clearly fit my management style. I knew that something was amiss, but I didn't know any other way to run the company. Then, one day, Christer Sandahl walked into my office. Christer was one of the people who had suddenly been "demoted" by my management style.

"What are you doing?" he asked me. "Why do you think you became the boss here? To be someone you aren't? No—you were made president because of who you *are*!"

Thanks to his courage and frankness, Christer helped me discover that my new role did not require me to change. The company was not asking me to make all the decisions on my own, only to create the right atmosphere, the right conditions for others to do their jobs better. I began to understand the difference between a traditional corporate executive, who issues instruction after instruction from the top, and the new corporate leader, who must set the tone and keep the big picture in mind. That conversation with Christer gave me the confidence to be myself and approach the job in a bold new way.

I had taken over at Vingresor during troubled times. The 1973–74 oil crisis had escalated air travel prices so much that passengers shied away from charter trips. It was our job to make Vingresor profitable again.

We didn't have many options. The main functions of a tour operator like Vingresor are to contract for flights and hotels and set up a service section at the travel resort that organizes excursions and activities. Then all these pieces are packaged together for the customer to purchase. The operator's profit is to a great extent a question of cost: the more money invested throughout the various stages of assembling the package, the smaller the profit margin and the greater the chances of losing money. The less invested, the less at risk.

In a sagging market, most production-oriented executives would have cut back on service. But this would only bring in less revenue, creating an even more serious problem. Instead, we chose to squeeze costs. At the time, we had about 210,000 customers, 40,000 of whom had purchased specially priced trips that were unprofitable to us. We decided to drive our costs down so that we could turn a profit even if we fell to 170,000 customers.

But we didn't just chop costs right off. We also restructured the organization, making it more flexible and able to handle more customers should the market bounce back. And the market truly did recover! Because of our flexibility, we easily absorbed the new customer demand and came out of the crisis showing a profit. During the first year of my presidency, we earned the largest profit in Vingresor's history.

## Linjeflyg

In 1978, when I'd been president of Vingresor for just under four years, I was offered the presidency of Linjeflyg, Sweden's domestic airline and an affiliate of SAS. I listened carefully to Nils Horjel, then chairman of the board of Linjeflyg, but I didn't seriously consider accepting his offer. A couple of days later I turned him down.

I didn't tell him what I was thinking, but to me, Linjeflyg was the greyest of grey. It operated domestic airline routes that catered to business executives who wanted to fly into Stockholm in the morning and home at night. Swedish political considerations kept fares to all points virtually identical. Corporate decisions were made mostly on the basis of which airplanes could perform most efficiently. Linjeflyg, and its preoccupation with filling seats at the lowest possible cost to the airlines, sounded to me like a typical pinstriped-suit company with no excitement whatsoever.

Nils Horjel accepted my answer with remarkable calm. "Okay, okay, we'll see," he said. It didn't sound as if he believed me. Only later did I learn that he was a former European handball star who had the cunning and determination to crack through the best defenses in the world. He called in his trump card, Curt Nicolin, a leading figure in Swedish industry and a member of the board, who then phoned me saying he wanted to talk about Linjeflyg. I still said no—two more times. Finally, he came to see me at my office.

In person, Curt took a different tack. Nils Horjel had painted a picture of a healthy Linjeflyg and assured me that the president's job would be worry free. But Curt realized that was exactly why I wasn't interested, and he described a much different company. "Things are pretty bad," he said.

Linjeflyg was losing money and desperately needed a strategy to turn it around. "We need you—and you alone—to step in and save the company," Curt said. Then he added an irresistible hook: the job would be the perfect challenge I needed to develop as an executive.

His ploy worked. I accepted the presidency of Linjeflyg, becoming, at 36, the youngest airline president in the world.

My first official act at Linjeflyg reaped benefits long afterward. My first day on the job I invited all the staff members, many of whom were stationed hours away, to Linjeflyg's main hangar at 11 A.M. I climbed a tall ladder and addressed the crowd from 15 feet off the ground.

"This company is not doing well," I said straightforwardly. "It's losing money and suffering from many problems. As the new president, I don't know a thing about Linjeflyg. I can't save this company alone. The only chance for Linjeflyg to survive is if you help me—assume responsibility yourselves, share your ideas and experiences so we have more to work with. I have some ideas of my own, and we'll probably be able to use them. But most important, *you* are the ones who must help *me*, not the other way around."

I sensed immediately that my speech was making a powerful impact. People left the meeting with a new spirit. They had never expected me to ask for their help. "We thought you were going to come and tell us what you were going to do," many employees told me later. "But you turned the tables on us!"

The experience proved to me once again that nobody was asking me to stand up there and tell everyone what to do. The people who worked for Linjeflyg were delighted to hear their "boss" ask them to participate actively in the company's future.

Before I arrived, the most discussed issue at Linjeflyg had been the uniforms of the female staff members—even though the airline had lost $3 million the year before, carried a passenger load of only 50 percent, and actually put its planes in the air only 4.8 hours a day (the international average was 7 hours). I saw this state of affairs as symptomatic of a company without a logical or company-wide strategy.

At the time, Linjeflyg was a classic product-oriented company. Ninety-five percent of its passengers were business travelers whose companies were basically resigned to paying the fares that Linjeflyg charged. The fares were determined by the airline's expenses, not by the demands and preferences of the market. The expenses stemmed from the size of the fleet, which was based on a self-imposed requirement that all the big cities in Sweden have a flight into Stockholm before 9 A.M. every weekday morning. Consequently, fares were high and standardized.

At the same time, the company had a conflict in objectives. No one had abandoned profit as an objective, but most of the management shared the political goal of forming a "rounder Sweden" in which even remote areas could enjoy convenient and affordable access to Stockholm. Thus, long journeys cost little more than short ones. This was terrific for the people of northern Sweden but not for Linjeflyg. My immediate priority, then, was to turn losses into profits. If nothing was done, the company faced certain bankruptcy.

Our first conclusion was that it's difficult to make money with an airplane that's sitting on the ground. We had to increase the number of flights and the only way to do that was to attract more passengers.

We already had Sweden's business travel market sewn up so we couldn't increase the actual number of business travelers. Instead, we had to induce them to fly more rather than opt for taking a train or driving, and the way to do that

was to offer more flights. And as for the non-business travelers who paid for the flights themselves, they seemed to be
taking the train, driving, or staying home. How could we
persuade them to start flying? By cutting prices, of course.

"Let's cut fares in half on those departures with low
passenger loads," I suggested. Our American consultant ad-
vised us against it, reminding us of some U.S. airlines that
had nearly gone broke using such a strategy. Fortunately, we
didn't listen to him.

Actually, the overall business strategy had four points
designed to convert Linjeflyg from a production-oriented
company into a customer-driven company. Using our fixed
resources better—that is, getting the planes up in the air more
hours per day— was only one of those points. A second one,
just as important, was to establish Linjeflyg as "the worlds
best airline" in terms of passenger service. And in Linjeflyg's
case, good service meant offering convenient timetables,
frequent departures, and low prices—not chateaubriand and
fine wines.

It is hard to explain to an American audience how
audacious talk of the "world's best airline" sounded in
Sweden in 1978. Swedes are not by nature brash. Historically,
it has been considered unseemly to call attention to oneself.
Even public praise or criticism is frowned upon. In saying that
we would become the "world's best airline," we were violat-
ing the social norm of moderation. For that reason, the impact
on our employees and on the public was tremendously
exciting.

The other two points of our business strategy, though
less visible to the public eye, were equally important in
transforming Linjeflyg into a customer-driven company. We
decided to spread responsibility among more people in the
organization and to streamline administrative resources
toward a more profit-oriented approach.

We gave the new organizational structure the shape of a heart: one half of the heart generated revenue and the other half incurred expenses. The basic idea was to let the market tell our marketing department what Linjeflyg should produce and sell. Then the marketing department would tell the operations department what to produce. In this way, we had turned the traditional organization on its head. Previously, the engineers had determined aircraft availability without taking into account when the customers wanted to fly. Instead of cutting service, as the engineers probably would have suggested, we would climb out of our financial hole by increasing revenue.

We presented our strategy package to the staff at a meeting in Stockholm. I began by explaining that Sweden had been transformed from a static, rural society into one that is vital and spread out. This transformation had created a new need for travel beyond the business transportation that Linjeflyg traditionally had provided. I then laid out the entire business strategy: the concept, the new organization, the new timetables and new fares, and even the ads. It was all very simple and logical—but I was stunned at the response.

The entire affair turned into a kind of revival meeting! When people left, "Love Is in the Air"—our new theme song—was playing on the loudspeakers, and everyone was talking about how exciting this new challenge was going to be. The reason for all this enthusiasm was that I had communicated with the staff very directly. Virtually everyone said to themselves, "That's exactly what I've always thought!"

I'll never forget the morning we initiated the new flights and new fares. Arriving at the departure terminal at Stockholm's Bromma Airport, I heard strains of "Love Is in the

Air" over the loudspeakers and saw the employees welcoming passengers to the "New Domestic Airline" with a warm smile and a red rose for each one.

Some people called this display "typical Carlzon," but the truth is that I hadn't arranged it—the employees had. In fact, when they found they couldn't hook the loudspeakers and the record player together, one employee voluntarily stood there all day holding a microphone in front of the tiny record player speaker. Everyone was working tremendously hard, but no one complained. On the contrary—they hadn't had this much fun at Linjeflyg in years!

From that day on, the number of passengers skyrocketed. And the variety of our passengers broadened substantially—not just businessmen but young people, retired people, and even families flew Linjeflyg.

Although we took a number of steps to improve the airline, the single most effective change was the dramatic cut in fares. If we hadn't lowered our fares enough, or hadn't promoted the reductions well, we wouldn't have reached any new people. We simply would have been lowering the fare for our established customers. To fill the planes in the middle of the day, we knew the off-peak fares had to be extremely low. We also knew that we would have to increase our advertising budget accordingly.

How much of a financial risk were we taking? I tried to calculate the potential loss on a single route, but the numbers were so enormous that I knew if I completed the estimate I wouldn't have the guts to try it. So I stopped calculating and let my intuition outweigh the mathematical computations.

"All Sweden at Half Price!" was the plain and simple message. And we also offered standby tickets to any destination in Sweden for about $20, a discount of 60 to 80 percent.

We invited SAS to join in this promotion on their domestic routes. The previous year, SAS and Linjeflyg had offered a youth fare called the Y50. The gist of it was that anyone under the age of 27 could get a 50-percent discount on a standby basis. That meant an airline ticket anywhere in Sweden would cost about $30. In considering a collaboration with us, SAS estimated that a further reduction in fare from $30 to $20 would draw 3,000 to 5,000 additional passengers—not enough to make up for the fare cut. They turned us down.

But we saw it through on our own. Since the $20 ticket price translated into 100 Swedish kronor, we called it the "Hundred Note" and featured the phrase in our advertising nationwide. Within weeks, thousands of young people with their backpacks were streaming to Bromma Airport in Stockholm, pitching tents and barbecuing hot dogs while waiting to get on a Linjeflyg flight. Our Hundred Note offer didn't attract just 5,000 more customers. It pulled in *125,000* the first summer alone!

Where did we get those 120,000 additional passengers that the SAS financial experts couldn't find in their calculations? The answer was simple: no one could figure out a Y50 discount, but everybody knew what a hundred note was. The story of the Hundred Note fare is proof that running a business is not always a matter of logic and mathematics. It's just as much a question of understanding the psychological impact that a new and intriguing offer will make on the market.

Another time we were reminded of how forceful a marketing influence psychology can be was when we pleased our customers by starting to charge them for breakfast. At a cost of about $400,000 a year, we had been serving a complimentary cup of coffee and a bun on all morning flights.

Virtually everyone complained about the quality of the coffee and the bun.

So we changed our approach. Instead of serving a free breakfast that no one liked, we decided to offer a full breakfast for about $2, half the cost of breakfast on a train. Passengers were quite willing to pay the price for a full breakfast, and we made 50 cents per serving.

Not everybody wanted a full breakfast; many had eaten before leaving home. "But if I could get a cup of coffee and a bun," they told us, "I'd be glad to pay a dollar for it."

So we began selling the breakfast that we used to give away. Our passengers who once complained were now happy, and we were bringing in more revenue.

From the employees themselves we received several other money-making ideas. One group of cabin attendants had long been requesting permission to sell chocolates, perfumes, and other items onboard. (Part of the reason was that they wanted more to do during the flight!) But the idea had run into a wall somewhere in the upper echelons of the company where a battery of studies had shown that it would be a money-loser. We threw out the studies but placed the challenge for success directly on the shoulders of the flight attendants: "You can try the project if you take financial responsibility for making the plan work. And if so, you will earn commissions on what you sell." They came back with a proposal that we accepted. We made millions from this venture, and the attendants earned hefty commissions.

The results tell the whole story: in the first year, we dropped our fares an average of 11 percent and our revenues increased from about $84 million to about $105 million. And without adding a single crew member or aircraft, we increased the number of passengers 44 percent simply by putting our planes up in the air more often.

All of this would have been impossible if we had stuck to the traditional way of working. If I had sat atop the pyramid issuing instructions we couldn't have executed our new plans in such a short time. And we probably wouldn't have hit upon a winning strategy, either, since so many of the successful ideas came from the employees themselves.

We surely could not have succeeded if so many employees had not been willing to devote extra time and effort to their jobs. What made them work so wholeheartedly? I think it was because they all understood our goals and strategies. We communicated a vision of what the company could be, and they were willing to take responsibility for making it work. For the first time, they saw something innovative happening at Linjeflyg and knew that success depended on them. They even read about their own company in the papers, which were enthusiastically reporting everything we were doing. Many times this media attention allowed us to leak plans before the details were completely worked out—an admittedly risky strategy but one that generated enormous energy inside the company.

In our advertisements, we openly compared our services to SJ, the Swedish railway, This was really unorthodox: not only were Swedes reluctant to toot their own horns, but there was a longstanding, unspoken agreement that the airlines wouldn't compete with the railroad for travelers. When the head of SJ asked me to stop, I told him things were different now—I was out to get his customers. Then he announced that SJ intended to counterattack with its own ads.

"Great!" I responded. "It's about time we had some competition. Sometimes it gets a little monotonous being a monopoly."

After a year of heated competition, he told me he'd changed his attitude. "Your ad campaign comparing yourselves with us was the best thing that could have happened to us," he said. "Suddenly everybody at SJ is yelling that we're going to prove that trains are better than planes any day!"

Vingresor, Linjeflyg, and SAS were three big Scandinavian companies, all connected with the travel industry, that I helped lead out of difficult times. Some people attribute my success to marketing gimmicks, but the truth is that I did not use the same program to solve the problems of these three very different companies. Rather, I succeeded because I reoriented each company toward the needs of the market it serves. To do this, I learned to rely more on the frontline people, who deal with the customers, and less on my own edicts. In other words, once I had learned how to be a leader rather than a manager, I was able to open up each company to new, market-oriented possibilities and to the creative energy of its employees.

# 3

# THE SAS TURNAROUND

In 1980, after two years at Linjeflyg, I was asked to take the job of chief operating officer of the airline in the SAS Group. By that time Linjeflyg was out of its own crisis and running smoothly. I also felt that I knew what was needed at SAS, so it was easy to say yes to the offer.

The entire airline industry was in trouble at the time. Major carriers had always experienced steady market growth year after year, but because of the oil crises during the 1970s, the market for both passengers and freight had finally stagnated. SAS, whose ownership is shared between private interests and the governments of Denmark, Norway, and Sweden, had a proud history of success, but when I took over, the company was in the midst of its second straight year of losing money. After 17 years of profit, SAS was headed toward a $20 million loss—a sizeable sum by Scandinavian standards—and everyone realized that something had to be done.

Many people at SAS assumed that I would cut fares dramatically, as I had done at Linjeflyg, and squeeze costs as much as possible, as I had done at Vingresor. But it wasn't that simple. At Vingresor we were faced with a slumping market, so we had to cut costs in order to make a profit on the customers we were able to retain. At Linjeflyg we had fixed costs, so we had to increase revenues; we did that by lowering fares and increasing the number of flights. But at SAS the situation was different—and required a different approach.

At first when the market stagnated, SAS executives assumed that revenues would not increase, and so they concentrated on cutting costs. For the 30 years between the end of World War II and the first oil crisis in 1973–1974, SAS had operated in a stable business environment with little competition. The company's annual revenues could be easily and reliably projected well in advance. The product, prices (allowing for inflation), and so on were fixed quantities, leaving the cost side as the only variable in the equation. To improve the bottom line, the obvious tactic was to close the gap between revenue and costs by cutting costs.

SAS's top management at the time used the standard weapon: the cheese slicer, which disregards market demands and instead cuts costs equally from all activities and all departments. The cheese slicer did succeed in cutting some costs that the company could forgo during a slump. But it also eliminated many services that customers wanted and were prepared to pay for while retaining others of little interest to the customers. In cutting costs, the company was, in effect, slicing away its own competitive strengths. The internal effects of the cuts were just as serious: staff members were sapped of their initiative. In the end, no one felt responsible for controlling costs.

During the initial period of my tenure at SAS, I was fortunate in having Helge Lindberg, one of our top executives, run the operation in consultation with some of the former managers. The new management team that I formed could then concentrate its time and energies on trying to steer SAS onto a new course.

The objective handed to us by the SAS board was to make the airline operation profitable even though the market couldn't be improved. We imposed one condition on ourselves: we would not achieve short-term profitability by selling airplanes, which so many airlines do in hard times. We would become profitable by providing the best service in the market, thereby increasing our share of the stagnant overall market.

We realized that SAS had already cut costs to the bone. Continuing to cut would have been like hitting the brakes of a car already standing still. You might push your foot through the floor of the car and cause permanent damage. Indeed, the only solution for SAS's predicament was to increase revenue.

First we needed a clear picture of the outside world and of SAS's position within it. Then we had to establish a goal and determine how to reach it. In other words, we had to create a new business strategy.

Our goal was for SAS to be profitable in its airline operations even in a zero-growth market such as we were then experiencing. The strategy we chose was to become known as "the best airline in the world for the frequent business traveler." We had pegged businessmen as the only stable part of the market. Unlike tourists, businessmen must travel in good times and bad. Perhaps most important, the business market has special requirements, and developing services to meet these requirements would enable us to attract their full-fare business.

This was not a fresh or particularly brilliant idea. All airlines know you cannot make a profit without attracting business travelers, because they are usually the only passengers who pay full fare. What was unique was the *way* we determined to achieve this goal. It was the opposite of the cheese-slicer approach.

We decided to stop regarding expenses as an evil that we should minimize and to begin looking at them as resources for improving our competitiveness. Expenses could, in fact, give us a competitive edge *if* they contributed to our goal of serving the business traveler.

So we scrutinized every resource, every expense, every procedure and asked ourselves, "Do we need this in order to serve the frequent business traveler?" If the answer was no, then we were prepared to phase out the expense or procedure, no matter what it was or how dear it was to those within the company. If the answer was yes, then we were prepared to spend *more* money to develop it further and make SAS more competitive. If something was missing, we were ready to add it. In other words, we decided to be one percent better at 100 things instead of being 100 percent better at one thing.

The result was a unique strategic plan for turning the company around. Far from cutting costs more, we proposed to the SAS board that we invest an *additional* $45 million and *increase* operating expenses $12 million a year for 147 different projects, including launching a comprehensive punctuality campaign, improving our traffic hub in Copenhagen, offering service courses for more than 12,000 of our staff, and restoring the olive in our customers' martinis. It was an enormous risk. We had no guarantee that these additional expenses would bring in more revenue. But it was also our only chance because the option of reducing costs had already been used.

Despite the high risk, the SAS board was enthusiastic. At a meeting in Denmark in June of 1981, the board accepted the plan unanimously and a few weeks later offered me the job of president of the SAS Group. So, in the midst of a stagnant market, at a time when we were losing close to $20 million a year, we gunned the throttle.

But it wasn't long before we also hit the brakes in some areas. Along the way we discovered a number of corporate policies and procedures that simply weren't contributing to our goal of serving business travelers. So at the same time that we were investing $45 million in the company, we undertook a huge project called Trim, which allowed us to cut $40 million.

Once we had identified the clear goal of serving business travelers, the cuts were easy to identify and we knew they wouldn't hurt us. For example, business travelers were not interested in helping us pay to maintain a department that promoted tourist trips or one that tried to bolster the position of the airline industry.

SAS had a 40-person market survey department that churned out extensive market analyses. The department served a vital function as long as all the decisions were made by a few executives isolated from the customers. But once we passed responsibility out to the front line, we no longer needed so many market surveys—our decisions were being made by people who had direct contact with the market all the time. So we gave those employees who had been immersed in statistics and computer printouts the opportunity to work out on the front line or to take direct responsibility for certain flight routes.

The same was true for paperwork. With responsibility so decentralized, we no longer needed as many people involved in writing instructions and policies, distributing them, and ensuring that they were obeyed. So we tossed out *all* the reports. Then we revived only the ones we discovered we really needed.

The whole plan was scheduled to be launched in the fall of 1981. During that summer the pieces were still a jumble, but they fell into place with surprising ease. Why? Not just because of the vision of top management but because people throughout the company were able to see that vision and take the initiative to put the pieces where they belonged. Wherever we did not have a system, the good sense and long experience of the employees saved a lot of time. People sometimes made mistakes, but there was nothing wrong with that. Mistakes can usually be corrected later; the time lost in not making a decision can never be retrieved.

The change in employee attitudes was one of the most significant results of the SAS turnaround strategy. By stating that we would turn a profit by becoming a service-oriented airline, we ignited a radical change in the culture at SAS. Traditionally, executives dealt with investments, management, and administration. Service was of secondary importance—the province of employees located way out on the periphery of the company. Now, the *entire* company—from the executive suite to the most remote check-in terminal—was focused on service.

The frontline employees' efforts were suddenly imbued with greater value within the company. All the employees received special training on providing service and, to many of them, the content of these courses was secondary to the fact that the company was investing time and resources in them. They had frequently gone unappreciated. Now they were in the limelight.

Beyond the attention to service, we were also able to stir new energy simply by ensuring that everyone connected with SAS—from board members to reservation clerks—knew about and understood our overall vision. As soon as we received approval from the board, we distributed a little red book entitled "Let's Get in There and Fight" to every one of our 20,000 employees. The book gave the staff, in very concise terms, the same information about the company's vision and goal that the board and top management already had. We wanted everyone in the company to understand the goal; we couldn't risk our message becoming distorted as it worked its way through the company.

There is no question that by diffusing responsibility and communicating our vision to all employees, we were making more demands on them. Anyone who is not given information cannot assume responsibility. But anyone who *is* given information cannot avoid assuming it. Once they understood our vision, our employees accepted responsibility enthusiastically, which sparked numerous simultaneous and energetic developments in the company. The media attributed most of these developments to me. But as the company was now organized, I was only one of thousands responsible for generating profits. The new energy at SAS was the result of 20,000 employees all striving toward a single goal every day.

In fact, few of our ideas were new. The previous management had already seen the need to become more service oriented. Many of the ideas we implemented had already existed in the form of studies and memorandums.

For example, there had long been talk within SAS of creating a special class for business travelers. This was hardly a novel idea; Air France, British Airways, and KLM had already inaugurated such programs. Now that SAS was dedicated to providing the best service for frequent business travelers, however, there was no question that we should institute a similar plan.

One of our problems was that too many SAS passengers were traveling on discount fares, not necessarily first class but full-fare coach as well. Other European airlines had created a business class by adding a surcharge to full-rate coach. We realized that we could improve our financial situation considerably merely by persuading more business travelers to pay full-fare coach prices. So, on our European flights, we dropped first class (which had mainly served as the world's most expensive dining room for airline executives anyway) and created "EuroClass," which offered considerably better service for full-fare coach prices. We retained our discount fares but did not promote them heavily at first because we were focusing on business travelers.

Having advertised better service for our EuroClass travelers, we then set out to provide it. First, we made the differences between the classes visible. We installed movable partitions on our aircraft to separate the EuroClass section from the others. At the terminals we provided comfortable lounges with telephone and telex services for EuroClass passengers. We gave business travelers separate check-in counters, more comfortable seats, and better food.

We also differentiated the level of service. EuroClass passengers were ushered through check-in in less than 6 minutes, as opposed to 10 for tourist class. Business travelers were allowed to board the plane last and disembark first. They received their meals first and were provided with free drinks, newspapers, and magazines.

The results were not long in coming. Our financial target had been to increase earnings by about $25 million in the first year, $40 million the second year, and $50 million the third year. To our amazement, we increased our earnings by nearly $80 million *the first year alone*—in a market that was slumping so drastically that other international airlines suffered combined losses of $2 billion. Within three years we had increased the number of full-fare passengers by 23 percent and discount passengers by 7 percent, even though the overall market was still stagnant. In 1985 and 1986, SAS's increases in passenger growth continued to outpace overall market growth.

Distinction came in other ways too. An August 1983 survey by *Fortune* named us the best airline for business travelers in the world. The respected trade publication *Air Transport World* named us "Airline of the Year" for 1983.

In a single year we had transformed a troubled airline with a morale problem, a slipping market share, and lots of red ink into exactly what we said it would become: the world's best airline for business travelers. And we were making a profit besides.

The profit itself, however, was not the most important thing. We might have been able to improve our results more than $80 million by cutting costs even more. But that would have been a short-term solution. It would have left us with dissatisfied passengers, an unmotivated staff, and an even lower market share. What was important was that we had achieved our new level of profitability by investing in the market, in the customers, and in the employees. The net result was not just an $80 million increase but millions of satisfied customers and thousands of motivated employees. In effect, we had acquired a major set of resources for the future.

# 4

# PROFESSION:  LEADER

In the summer of 1981, the first year I became president of SAS, I decided to take two weeks' vacation. But as soon as I arrived at my country house, the telephone began ringing. And it kept right on ringing with questions from people back at the office about the most mundane matters. Of course, sitting out in the country, I possessed less information than anyone at headquarters about what was going on, but they called me anyway. After a couple of days I gave up and returned to Stockholm. It was a waste of time to try to do my job long distance.

The following summer, a Swedish newspaper asked to interview me on the subject of "taking it easy." I agreed, but only on the condition that the article be published a week *before* my vacation. I wanted to make sure that everybody at SAS read what I had to say.

In the interview, I explained that I believed responsibility should be delegated within a company so that individual decisions are made at the point of responsibility, not far up the organizational chart. I said that we had created an organization designed to work in this manner and had appointed managers who were expected to operate this way. "Now I intend to take four weeks' vacation," I stated. "If my telephone *doesn't* ring, that is proof that I have succeeded—people have accepted responsibility and are making decisions on their own. But if the phone rings, then I have failed—either in getting my message across or in recruiting managers who can accept responsibility."

A few days later I left for vacation. And for four weeks, the telephone remained wonderfully silent.

That was the best evidence that the organization was, indeed, working the way it was designed to work—even if I had helped things along a little with the interview. Upon my return, I discovered that many decisions had been made in my absence. Some of them didn't thrill me—I probably would have chosen differently—but the significant accomplishment was that decisions had been made. Other people were taking responsibility based on accurate, up-to-date information.

That is the difference between the traditional business manager and the true leader in a customer-driven company. I like to think that the successes at Linjeflyg and SAS came about largely because I took to heart the important lessons I had learned early on at Vingresor. A leader is not appointed because he knows everything and can make every decision. He is appointed to bring together the knowledge that is available and then create the prerequisites for the work to be done. He creates the systems that enable him to delegate responsibility for day-to-day operations.

In the past, of course, it would have been inconceivable for the president of a company to cut himself off from the office completely for a month. A top manager was expected to make all the important decisions himself so he was always directly involved in operations. Important decisions had to be made constantly, and he therefore expected to work day and night, weekdays and weekends. Saying "I haven't been able to take a real vacation in four years" showed his firm control and indispensability.

The typical chief executive was a decision-making machine. Employees supplied the raw data about a problem and presented their alternative solutions. The chief executive then processed this information and spewed forth the answer: "We'll take Alternative 2B." Since he was the only one who saw the overall picture, he was compelled to make important decisions himself. No one else was equipped to do so.

This system made it look as if the chief executive was taking full responsibility, but actually almost the opposite was true. He was not taking responsibility for the most crucial part of his job: making sure that the overall vision of the company was achieved. He was only making decisions about those issues that came to his attention. But even if all the important matters made their way up the pyramid, and even if the executive was a consummate decision-maker, he simply had *no time* to investigate every issue and render an informed judgment.

What were the results? Many decisions were simply never made. No one in the company was able to keep in mind the overall vision—the staff because they weren't privy to it, and the chief executive because he got too bogged down in decision-making. And many employees became passive, believing that even if they were to come up with a good idea, "management wouldn't let us do it anyway."

Many people consider it extremely demanding to manage in this classic fashion—they are constantly imposed upon by their staff, and they must work through nights, weekends, and vacations. But I believe the job of a true leader is actually much more difficult.

Nobody puts a proposal for a new comprehensive strategy on your desk and asks you to make a decision about it. You have to put it there yourself. And once you use your view of the big picture to formulate a strategy, you have to call on a wide range of skills to achieve a series of objectives. You must devise a business strategy tailored to your goal. You need to communicate the goal and strategy to the board of directors, the unions, and all the employees. You have to give greater responsibility to people at the front line and then create a secure atmosphere where they will dare to use their new authority. You must build an organization that can work to achieve the goal and establish measures that guarantee you are moving in the right direction. In short, you have to create the prerequisites for making the vision a reality.

This is a lot harder than implementing it yourself. I made exactly that mistake when I first became president of SAS. Though passenger business was our primary emphasis, we had also given our air cargo people responsibility for developing a new strategy. But it seemed to me that they were just coming up with general rallying cries like "Go, Cargo, Go." I was impatient and eager for some "real" strategic thinking.

So I sat down with the head of cargo operations and said, "This can't be so difficult. What the market wants, of course, is door-to-door service. Develop such a product and call it EuroCargo which will fit together nicely with our EuroClass on the passenger end."

He obeyed and, as you've probably guessed, it was a big flop. Why? Because I had made a decision from the top of the pyramid about an aspect of the business that was completely unfamiliar to me. I lacked a basic knowledge of the cargo market's special structure and division of labor. Coming from the passenger end, I did not understand that cargo was different—that it is a heavy industrial product sold to major manufacturing corporations through long-term contracts.

If I had created an atmosphere in which the cargo managers' own ideas flourished, of course, the mistake would not have been made. Instead, I took the easy way out, opting to decide myself, even though I didn't know what I was doing.

Many executives make that same choice, apparently believing that they cannot be good managers unless they know—or pretend to know—everything. Peoples' whispers that their immediate superior "doesn't know anything—he couldn't even do my job," are strong evidence that their boss thinks he has to know it all.

But a business executive need not have detailed, specialized knowledge. I am the president of a large airline, but I can neither fly a plane nor repair one—and no one at SAS expects me to. A leader today must have much more general qualities: good business sense and a broad understanding of how things fit together—the relationships among individuals and groups inside and outside the company and the interplay among the various elements of the company's operations.

What is required is strategic thinking, or "helicopter sense"—a talent for rising above the details to see the lay of the land. The ability to understand and direct change is crucial for effective leadership. Today's business leader must manage not only finances, production, technology, and the like but also human resources. By defining clear goals and strategies and then communicating them to his employees and training them to take responsibility for reaching those goals, the leader can create a secure working environment that fosters flexibility and innovation. Thus, the new leader is a listener, communicator, and educator—an emotionally expressive and inspiring person who can create the right atmosphere rather than make all the decisions himself.

These skills were once regarded as feminine, an association that goes back to women's roles in the old agricultural society when they took care of family and social relationships in the village. Their intuition and sensitivity to other people's situations are traits that are essential for any manager but cannot, unfortunately, be picked up overnight.

The new leadership role should open up many more possibilities for women in business. When we hired Birgitta Rydbeck as director of the SAS Flight Academy, we were looking for a professional *manager*, not a long-time pilot. Birgitta had a degree in business administration, and we were confident that she could create the proper conditions for flight training. Our move caused quite a stir among the pilots who believed that a specialist in aviation technology should have the position. They were quick to come around, though, as Birgitta demonstrated the perfect blend of leadership traits and proved herself a capable manager. I firmly believe that, in the long run, men and women alike will benefit from using "feminine" and "masculine" qualities in good combination.

In many respects, though, the leader has to be an enlightened dictator—one who is willing to disseminate the vision and goals throughout a large, decentralized organization but who will not brook active dissent to the underlying ideas. He must be able to present his vision convincingly so that the goals and strategies feel right to everyone in the company. Indeed, as my experience at Linjeflyg and SAS shows, the management's vision often corresponds with the employees' own ideas.

Some employees may not see or fully understand the vision and goals at the beginning. The leader must resist the urge to dismiss those people and, instead, work with them, give them additional information, and attempt again to make them understand.

Of course, there will always be those who refuse to be persuaded. From them, he must demand loyalty, if not emotional commitment, to the goals. Otherwise, they should be asked to leave.

At SAS we were able to convince almost every employee of the value of our vision. Everyone aligned and began moving enthusiastically in the same direction, and we were able to stir up a pretty strong wind, as our profit-and-loss statement showed. However, if one in ten had gone in a different direction, the countermovement would have slowed the momentum at a crucial moment in the company's history.

Therefore, when I say we must collapse the hierarchical structure in service-oriented businesses, I am not calling for corporate democracy in its purest form. Certainly, everyone—middle management, frontline employees, union leaders, and board members—must be given the opportunity to air their views and ideas. But they cannot all be involved in making every final decision.

The board of directors appoints the president and the top management team to design, present, and pursue a business strategy. Only after the leader has fully developed this strategy and communicated it to everyone else can he begin delegating responsibility—as he *must* do in a customer-driven company. A leader is one who creates the right environment for business to be done.

In the game of soccer, the coach is a leader whose job it is to select the right players. He must also ensure that his team goes onto the field in the best condition to play a good game. On the field, there is a team captain, analogous to a manager, with the authority to issue orders on the field and to change plays during the course of the game. But most important are the individual players, each of whom becomes his own boss during the game.

Imagine a situation in which a soccer player breaks away toward an open goal and suddenly abandons the ball to run back to the bench and ask the coach for the order to kick the ball into the goal. Before he can run back to the ball, he has lost not only the ball but also the game.

In changing a business environment, you can't wield total control from the top of a pyramid. You must give people authority far out on the line where the action is. They are the ones who can sense the changes in the market. By giving them security, authority, and the right to make decisions based on current market conditions, you put yourself in the best position to gain a competitive edge.

A leader, then, is a person who is oriented toward results more than power or social relations. Someone seeking power for its own sake may well sacrifice both personal relationships and results to obtain it. Someone who is too socially oriented might tend to compromise at every turn in order to avoid conflict. In the long run, this hurts results. But the results-oriented leader does not dictate the methods for achieving the results and, moreover, does not need to claim the victories as his own.

At times, the press in Scandinavia has "divulged" that I personally have not originated all the ideas that have led to SAS's success. I welcome these revelations because they highlight exactly what I've been saying all along. The great triumph at SAS is that we have unleashed our employees' creativity through decentralization. Good ideas flow freely from every division of the company and are all channelled toward the same company-wide vision.

The same applies to my approach to outside consultants. I have frequently heard it whispered that in actuality a consultant thought up a particular idea. It seems to be a point of honor to be able to handle a situation without having to turn to outside consultants. That is something that I have never really understood. It must spring from the traditional view that the manager has superior, infallible knowledge and must always retain total control.

To me, it cannot be anything other than sensible and responsible to bring a ship's pilot on board when you are steering your vessel into new and dangerous waters!

For a manager who wants to make all the decisions himself at all levels of the company, it may not be as prestigious to bring in an outside consultant who would then be involved in making some of these decisions. On the other hand, if you reorganize along the lines that I have set down here, then you may have to change the overall direction of the company. This is like trying to get a battleship to change course, a process that requires tremendous amounts of energy and very special skills.

If the leader now delegates responsibility to people throughout the company in order to bring about this change, then it would be unreasonable to expect that each could be a specialist in every aspect of it. Their job is to cope with long-term development far after the change has been completed. If I give them responsibility, then I also have to let them bring in the extra resources they need—a financial expert, an organizational consultant, or an advertising agency.

It makes no difference who comes up with good ideas. All that matters is that the ideas have worked, and today SAS is a strong organization that serves its customers well.

# 5

# SETTING THE STRATEGY

$S$ome time ago I sat down with the president of a U.S.-based airline to discuss a joint venture—providing a terminal at one of the major U.S. airports to link our respective flights and passenger handling systems. Determined to make it the best passenger service terminal in the country, we were willing to invest $60-70 million in the venture. Our contacts in the other airline had seemed equally enthused, and both of our staffs had spent considerable time laying the groundwork before our meeting.

After five minutes, I could see that my prospective partner wasn't interested in making an investment in better service for his passengers. He stated flatly that a terminal shouldn't be a "fancy palace," just a bunker. He then quickly changed the subject to the latest advances in aviation technology. Though I listened for another half hour, I knew this wasn't a company we wanted to do business with.

Not long thereafter I visited Bob Crandall, chief executive officer of American Airlines, to find out how his company was tackling the deregulated U.S. marketplace. Bob explained how he was positioning his company in the market; how American had built up a hub-and-spoke system; how the company had developed its information and communications system to secure access to the market; how he worked with the unions; and how he spent 30 percent of his time communicating with his employees.

After two hours it struck me that he still had not mentioned anything about airplanes. Finally, I prodded him by asking what kind of planes he was buying these days. He looked at me in amazement—almost as if he didn't understand what I was saying. "Airplanes?" he asked. "What are you talking about? We buy whatever we need to do business."

I hardly have to add that while the first company is now bathing in red ink, American remains one of the most profitable airlines in the country. Why the dramatic difference in fortunes? The first airline executive was mired in a production-oriented philosophy. Bob Crandall, on the other hand, understood that to survive under deregulation, U.S. airlines would have to learn to serve their customers better. Then he set out a business strategy to ensure that American would be a customer-driven company.

Unlike his counterpart at the other airline, Bob Crandall had taken those crucial first steps that many leaders ignore. He assessed the business climate and determined the needs of his customers. Based on that knowledge, he outlined a business strategy to meet the customers' needs within the context of the marketplace and organized his company intelligently to carry out that strategy.

Remarkably, many business executives begin by devising goals and strategies, and only later back into an examination of the business climate and the customers' needs. Obviously, this is proceeding in the wrong order. How can you know what your goals or strategies should be if you don't have a clear picture of the environment you're working in or of what your customers want? Sadly, by the time many businesses recognize they should have planned the other way around, it's too late.

Given today's increased competitiveness and emphasis on service, the first step must be to acquire a customer orientation. To a certain extent, this means looking at your company and deciding, from the customer's point of view, what business you're really in. For example, is SAS in the airline business? Or is it really in the service business, to transport people from one place to another in the safest and most efficient way possible? I think it's obvious that the answer is the latter.

The response to that question will go a long way toward determining how you will organize your company to provide the best service. Are Ford and General Motors in the automobile business? Or are they really in the business of providing people with the means to transport themselves from one place to another overland? If they decide they are in the automobile business, then naturally they should concentrate their efforts on state-of-the-art design and aerodynamics and fuel economy—on the car itself.

But let us say they decide they are in the ground transport service business. Does this mean they have to sell cars at all? Wouldn't it also make sense—from the customer's point of view—to sell a plastic card guaranteeing that a car would be made available to you immediately, wherever and whenever you want to drive somewhere? After all, when you call for a taxi, you don't specify a Ford or Chevrolet taxi. You're ordering a transportation service.

I am not suggesting that Ford and General Motors ought to stop concentrating on cars. But I think the point is clear: when you are oriented toward your customers, you are probably in the business of providing them with a service in addition to the "hardware" itself.

Similarly, banks are no longer in the business of handling coins and notes. Now their business centers on managing the information flow about economic transactions. I suspect that any banker who has not redefined his services accordingly will soon be out of business.

Once you determine who your customers are, you can decide what business you're really in. This sounds easy, but for those sitting at the top of the pyramid—and not working on the front lines, in day-to-day contact with the customers—it can be tricky.

At Vingresor, we realized that senior citizens were becoming an important category of consumers in the travel business. So we worked out a comprehensive approach to attract them to our tour packages.

We—that is, a team of managers like me, just over 30 years old—concluded that senior citizens were fearful of traveling abroad and therefore would want to stay in special hotels filled only with other Swedish senior citizens. No doubt, they would prefer an apartment-type suite with a living room where they could entertain their new friends and a kitchen equipped with a special Swedish coffeemaker and Swedish coffee. The social rooms would, of course, have a plentiful supply of Swedish board games and playing cards.

We knew that the tour conductors needed to have some form of medical training and that they should be solid, down-to-earth people—probably ruddy-cheeked, matronly nurses. Special arrangements would be made with a few nearby restaurants to serve Scandinavian dishes suited to our guests' cranky stomachs. And since we assumed that older people prefer getting out and seeing the sights to sunbathing on the beaches, we arranged a wealth of brief excursions, interspersed with plenty of restroom breaks.

We were quite satisfied with our new product but decided to find out what the seniors themselves thought. So we invited a group of about 15 from a Stockholm retirement club for coffee and cookies. We barely sat down when the first one spoke up.

"I just had to tell you that I thought it was crazy that you left Nueva Suecia down at the beach in St. Augustin and instead moved the whole kit and caboodle up to Monto Rojo on the other side of the road," she said. "After all, when we're visiting the Canary Islands, we want to be right at the beach, not sitting beside a hotel pool."

Fine, we thought. This little old lady is an unusually experienced traveler. She can't represent the entire group.

Immediately another woman added, "I don't understand why you've shut down Medaro and started with Los Christianos and Playa las Americos on the south coast of Tenerifa. Medaro was more exciting and more primitive, and that's what suits me best."

All right, we thought. So she doesn't represent the group either.

Then a gentleman explained, "This is what I do when I travel. I look for a cheap trip in the newspaper ads—never more than a week, mind you, because then it gets tiresome. When I get back home, I pick up the paper and begin looking for another cheap trip so I can take off again."

By now we were beginning to wonder just who these people were.

Then we heard from another one: "Mexico—that's a place I think you should include. We've been to Sri Lanka and Gambia and everywhere else, but Mexico seems *really* fascinating."

And so it continued, until finally not a single retiree there expressed interest in our wonderful product. We thanked them for coming to Vingresor and promptly dismissed all of their opinions. We stubbornly invested $100,000 in beautiful, tabloid-size brochures with huge block letters. And our matronly nurses were left waiting for pensioners who never showed up.

That's what happens when you sit at the top of the pyramid, far from the reality of the market, and you develop a product you think will please your customers. If we'd started by believing the seniors—or listening to our experienced sales staff and tour conductors who knew them—we probably would have ended up mixing the pensioners with the young adults at a hotel that caters to an active lifestyle.

After you discover what your customers really want, you can turn to establishing your business goals and a strategy to achieve them. These goals needn't be complicated. But whatever they are, they should be oriented toward the customer, and you should use them as a yardstick against which to measure your strategy and results.

When I came to SAS in 1981, we set a goal to become the world's best airline for the business traveler. At the time, SAS had just taken delivery of four Airbuses—large, short-haul planes that were technologically modern and had bright, spacious interiors. The four Airbuses alone had cost $120 million and we had ordered another eight.

Such a large purchase was not unusual for a major airline. Since the beginning of commercial aviation, SAS and all of its counterparts had regularly replaced their aircraft with newer, more technologically advanced models that could fly passengers at a lower cost per seat mile to the airlines. It was an article of faith among airline executives that new aircraft should be purchased as soon as they were available.

The Airbuses could be operated six percent more cheaply per passenger mile than the DC-9, our workhorse aircraft. But the Airbuses were also bigger than the DC-9s (240 seats vs. 110 seats), so no savings could be realized unless the Airbuses flew with a full passenger load. And after making the purchase, SAS discovered that its passenger base was too small.

The Airbuses had been purchased based on forecasts that our passenger load would increase from seven to nine percent annually and that cargo would increase rapidly as well. But, with the onslaught of the oil crisis, the market had stagnated. The only economical way for SAS to fly Airbuses from Stockholm to major cities in continental Europe was to fill them up in Copenhagen. They were too big to provide nonstop service from other Scandinavian cities to continental Europe—a service our customers were demanding.

To airline executives who assumed that their passenger market would grow steadily each year the approach of constantly investing in new aircraft made sense—and, indeed, it had helped SAS chalk up 17 consecutive profitable years. But we could no longer afford that kind of thinking now that the market had plateaued. We had to start taking the point of view of our customers, the business travelers. And seen from their perspective, the picture looked very different.

We saw that the only way SAS could use the Airbus economically was to provide poor service to the very customers we were working to attract. How would business executives in Stockholm and elsewhere in Scandinavia prefer to organize their travels? Would they want to fly in our roomy, new Airbuses, even if they would have few flights to choose from and required stops in Copenhagen? Or would they prefer traveling in ordinary DC-9s on frequent, nonstop flights from Stockholm, Oslo, or elsewhere directly to major cities in continental Europe?

To me, the answer was obvious. "Put the Airbuses in mothballs," I said. "Use the DC-9s instead."

Many people at SAS were aghast; it was as if a company had built a brand new factory, only to have the president close it down on dedication day. But it was the decision that made the most sense. I wasn't saying Airbuses aren't fine aircraft; they are. In fact, we have leased them for charter excursions since we stopped using them on our own routes. But to remain competitive in attracting the limited market of Scandinavian business travelers, we had to offer frequent, nonstop flights. And we couldn't do that using the Airbuses.

The Airbus story illustrates the difference between a production-oriented philosophy and a customer-driven philosophy. The classic production-oriented company produces or invests—in this case by purchasing an aircraft—and adapts its operations to the equipment.

In the early days of air travel, there was nothing wrong with this orientation. Flying was still an event that people considered worth some inconvenience; they weren't seeking good service as much as a novel experience. And it was genuinely important for airlines to keep up with aircraft development because each new model represented enormous productivity gains. During this period the "flag carrier" concept emerged. Airlines from each nation flew to as many destinations as possible just to put their country's flag there, even if they scheduled only one flight a week.

If a Scandinavian business executive wanted to fly on SAS to Chicago or Rio in 1960, for example, he would plan his trip around our available flights. A loyal SAS customer was perfectly willing to defer to our schedules. The alternative modes of transportation took much longer, and some national pride was involved in his choice of airlines.

Today it works in reverse. When a business traveler plans a trip, he arranges his meetings and then books a flight on the airline that best suits his timetable. If SAS has a convenient flight, he'll fly with us; otherwise, he won't. So SAS now focuses on those destinations that have enough passengers to support frequent flights, daily and nonstop—and that is why we cannot use large planes like theAirbus or the 747. Our new customer-oriented perspective starts with the market instead of the product. Then the means of production is tailored to give the customers the best possible products.

Just as we mothballed the Airbuses, we decided to increase our fleet of DC-9s even though a new generation of planes was available. We had studied them all, but no new plane was better suited for business traveler demands, or more profitable for SAS, than the DC-9s we already flew. Our decision was so unconventional that even I felt a little uncertain. I asked executives at another airline, "How do you decide to buy new planes? Will they be more profitable than the planes you already have? Or will they improve your service?"

My question puzzled them. "Well, we never looked at it that way. It was so obvious we should buy new planes that we never compared them with the old ones. We've always done it that way."

Once we had decided not to buy new planes, we knew that we had plenty of time before we would need to replace our fleet. When we began to study the available planes, we noticed that there had been some dazzling technical advances yet there were surprisingly few refinements in the cabin where the passengers were located. We had the time to develop a new plane that would really be right for us and our customers.

Although well into the 1970s a plane's economic lifetime was much shorter than its technical lifetime (in other words, it was profitable to replace planes long before they wore out), in the seventies and eighties it has been the other way around: a plane's economic lifetime is longer than its technical lifetime; and so there are seldom any economic reasons to replace planes.

Customers' reactions to the new planes of the early 1980s seemed to bear out our decision. Lufthansa recently switched to a fleet of sleek, new Boeing 737s. These planes may have been technologically advanced, but to the customer there was only one striking change: instead of having rows with three seats on one side of the aisle and two seats on the other, as in a DC-9, there were three seats on each side. In other words, there were more *middle* seats.

When was the last time anyone asked for a middle seat before boarding a flight? Why did Lufthansa make that $600 million investment? It appears that Lufthansa regards airplane purchases purely in terms of production technology. Of the new planes on the market, the 737 was certainly the best alternative. But buying new planes shouldn't be equated with doing good business in a service company.

Knowing that our DC-9s would be in operation for a few more years, we realized that we had time to design an airplane with something really new in terms of passenger comfort—something that would at least give us a substantial competitive advantage over other airlines. Obviously, we wanted the best technology, too, but what we were really looking for was what we called the "Passenger Pleasing Plane," or the "3-P." Our senior management proposed that our goal should be to build an aircraft that, for the first time since the DC-3 50 years ago, would feature real innovations in the passenger cabin such as more space to store carry-on luggage, wider twin aisles and doors for easier mobility onboard and in disembarking, no middle seats, and reduced cabin noise.

The SAS board agreed, and three of us—Curt Nicolin, our chairman; Frede Ahlgreen Eriksen, our executive vice president; and I—made the rounds of aircraft manufacturers to discuss the matter. We soon realized why the Three-P plane had never been produced. Like any other business, airplane manufacturers had to please their customers—the airlines. And airline executives were so caught up in technological innovations that they hardly gave a thought to making the passenger's ride more comfortable.

One of the plants we visited was Boeing in Seattle, where we met with the entire top management group. They had orchestrated a slick presentation, including color pictures of new planes with the SAS insignia already emblazoned on them. We listened politely, then informed Boeing that we were not interested in their current planes. We wanted something else. We wanted a plane that for the first time ever would be tailored to the needs of the passenger. After all, that is who pays to fly in the plane.

They listened to us, but I suspected that they didn't take us seriously. Finally, they asked what we "really" meant. At that point, Curt Nicolin, an engineer by training, sketched a traditional airplane on a napkin. He drew a cross-section of the oval-shaped fuselage. The floor of the cabin is located at the widest part of the oval—the midpoint. That means only 50 percent of the fuselage space is used for passengers.

"Turn the oval on its side," Nicolin said. "Then put the floor on the bottom, not halfway up. That way you can use 80 percent of the space for passengers."

"Interesting," our hosts politely responded. Then they talked about air resistance and enumerated all the other technical reasons it couldn't be done.

But a few weeks later the chairman of Boeing phoned to say that he absolutely had to meet with me in Paris during the biennial air show there. When I saw him, he eagerly pulled a huge stack of drawings out of his briefcase. After our visit to Seattle, he explained, the Boeing executives had told their designers about our fuzzy and somewhat naive ideas for building an airplane. The designers immediately opened their file drawers and hauled out one drawing after another showing fascinating ideas for improving the passenger environment.

"Why haven't you shown these to us before?" the executives asked.

"No one asked for them," the designers replied. In fact, they had sketched their ideas on their own time, more or less covertly, because they too believed the development of a better passenger environment had been neglected.

In 1985 we joined Boeing in a project to develop new, passenger-oriented aircraft for use in the 1990s—just about the time when our DC-9s will finally reach the end of their useful life. By now, the Three-P Plane concept is familiar throughout the airline industry and is sure to leave its mark on the next generation of airplanes.

This story again illustrates the gap between a customer-driven and a production-oriented approach. Manufacturers have long talked technology with technicians. Every design change has centered on achieving the lowest possible operating cost per seat per mile. It had not occurred to anyone that a change in the shape of the product might generate new revenue, even if the unit cost were not the lowest in absolute terms.

I am not saying that Boeing's top management team was obdurate. They had done their best to meet their clients' demands. Nor had these clients—the airline executives—done their job incorrectly. They had become accustomed to working in a market where growth was rapid and competition was limited. But today the situation is different, so we must think along new lines.

As I learned more about SAS, I was amazed at how many of its policies and procedures catered to the equipment or the employees, even if they inconvenienced the passengers. Equally amazing was how easy these practices were to spot—and to rectify—by looking at them from the point of view of our target customer, the frequent business traveler.

Early one morning I arrived at Copenhagen Airport on the flight from New York and had to change planes to get to Stockholm. I had plenty of hand baggage, and I was tired from flying all night. Once inside the terminal, I looked around the concourse for the Stockholm gate. There were planes bound for Los Angeles, Chicago, and Rio but none for my destination.

So I asked an SAS employee where the Stockholm gate was. He said that it was in Concourse A—a half mile away.

"But why isn't it right here?" I asked. "All of us are going on to Stockholm."

Eyeing me with a slight air of superiority he retorted, "Only wide-body planes park here."

"I see," I said. "You mean to say there are a lot of passengers here in Copenhagen who get off the plane from New York and then immediately board the plane to Chicago? Is that why all the wide-bodies are next to each other?"

"No, no." he answered. "They're here because they're all serviced at the hangar right over there."

"But why is my plane at the other end of the airport?" I asked.

"Well, that's because it was operating on Danish domestic routes in the morning and Concourse A is closest to the domestic terminal."

I tried to explain to him that I was standing here right now, not in Concourse A, and it would be nice if my plane were here too.

The problem was that the planes were being positioned at the departure gate that was most convenient for the planes! The ground handlers chose the departure gate closest to the hangar or the gate where the plane had arrived.

Now, I've heard many a business traveler swear up and down about having to rush around between the concourses at Copenhagen Airport—but I've never heard an airplane complain about being dragged a couple of hundred yards. Today at Copenhagen we tow more planes from concourse to concourse. Whereas once two-thirds of our passengers in transit had to change concourses at Copenhagen, that figure is down to one-third. Not only are our passengers less harried but we've minimized delays caused by waiting for passengers who needed a few extra minutes to dash from one concourse to another.

Another example of how we allowed customers' preferences to guide our decisions was when we established a nonstop route from Stockholm to New York, even though we couldn't use our most impressive airliner for the flight.

For years, SAS had flown to New York two ways: from Stockholm via Oslo, using a Boeing 747, and nonstop from Copenhagen. When we reoriented the company toward the business traveler—whose highest priority is convenience, not price—we added a nonstop Stockholm to New York flight using the DC-10.

We decided to try two such flights a week, though on paper such a route looked unprofitable. Within two months, however, the Stockholm-New York nonstop had become the most profitable route in our long-haul network. We were determined to find out why.

It turned out that on the days when Stockholm-New York travelers would have had to change in Copenhagen or stop in Oslo on SAS, they took another airline instead. They flew from Stockholm to London or Amsterdam and changed there—particularly if their ultimate U.S. destination was other than New York and they could get a direct flight from continental Europe.

But on the days when SAS flew nonstop from Stockholm to New York in the smaller DC-10, not a single Scandinavian business traveler was abandoning SAS.

One often neglected challenge of developing a business strategy is knowing when to say no to good ideas that don't fit. I remember once asking the late Simon Spies, a sage of the Scandinavian package tour business, why he didn't offer any attractive vacation discounts or special services for children.

"There's nothing wrong with kiddie clubs and all that sort of thing," he said. "But the point is that, in this company, we've decided that what we're selling is vacations for grown-ups—good, simple tour packages for individuals or couples. Children's clubs don't fit into that strategy."

Raising his forefinger, he continued: "Jan, never forget that the hardest part of making good business deals is to resist making bad business deals. I don't care about all the families with children who pass us by, as long as we've decided that we want to do business with another category of customer and are willing to go the extra mile for them."

SAS receives a hundred business offers and proposals a month, many of them quite good. But only a fraction fit in with our goal of providing the best possible service for the frequent business traveler. The rest would require us to dissipate our energy after we have worked so hard to focus it on our goal.

For example, every self-respecting airline is supposed to be represented at the annual international tourist industry convention in San Diego. One year, 20 SAS employees signed up to attend out of sheer habit, but we turned them down. Why should we be interested in a tourist industry convention? It didn't fit in with our business-travel strategy.

Another time, we received permission to fly our Scandinavian-Tokyo route over Siberia. We were quite excited because it meant cutting five hours off the trip, which we anticipated would attract more business travelers.

Then someone suggested that the return trip should take the longer route, with a stopover in Anchorage. His argument was that the plane could then arrive in Scandinavia in the early morning. That way, Japanese tourist groups could begin their first day with sightseeing and save the first night's hotel expenses.

This was actually a very good idea, except for one thing: it had nothing to do with our strategy of targeting business travelers. In fact, it was detrimental to it. Business executives don't want to spend five unnecessary hours in an airplane and arrive wrinkled and tired just when they have to rush off to a business meeting. They would much rather fly the shortest route, arrive in the evening, and pay for a good night's sleep in a hotel.

In contrast to a production-oriented company, where decisions are motivated by product and technology considerations, the customer-oriented company begins with the market and lets *it* guide every decision, every investment, every change.

If we had chosen to be "The Tourist Airline," we would never have mothballed the Airbuses or kept our DC-9s or introduced the DC-10 nonstop service from Stockholm to New York or frowned on the idea of a stopover in Anchorage. We would have brought new and larger planes, scheduled fewer departures, and attracted more Japanese tourists—all of which would have given us lower costs per passenger mile and also lower fares. Tourists are perfectly willing to wait a day or two as long as the price is low enough. But we had targeted business travelers, and they would rather pay than be inconvenienced. Having targeted them, giving them what they wanted enabled us to remain clearly focused on our chosen strategy.

Our concentration on the business travel market does not mean that we have forgotten or disregarded the tourist market. Just the opposite, in fact. There is an important paradox here: the more we do for business travelers, the easier it becomes to offer low prices to tourist travelers.

The more discretionary tourist-class travelers we attract to fill otherwise empty seats, the higher the revenue per flight. Invariably, however, there are empty seats on flights that, due to the day of travel or departure time, are not attractive to business travelers. Since we generally have a high percentage of full-fare travelers, and those full fares have paid what it actually costs to operate a flight, we can afford to "dump" prices on the empty seats. By substantially discounting the seats the business travelers don't want, we stand to make even more money per flight. If we sell every seat, our overall revenue is greater and we can pass the extra earnings on to business travelers by lowering fares for them as well. And, what's more, those discount fares don't have to be rock-bottom as long as they are low enough to fill every empty coach seat at any given time.

That's just what we've done. SAS has the highest percentage of full-fare travelers and the lowest tourist-class fares in Europe today. And the benefits ultimately circle back to our primary market, the business traveler.

# 6

# FLATTENING THE PYRAMID

A few years ago, Werner Tarnowski was appointed to manage the SAS office in Stuttgart. Inheriting an outmoded organizational structure, Werner set three major goals: (1) to cut costs without sacrificing the quality of service, (2) to increase the efficiency of his staff, and (3) to give the organizational structure more flexibility.

The Stuttgart branch operated out of two locations: a ticket sales office downtown, where Werner and other district managers worked, and the airport itself, where the flight-related personnel reported.

The downtown office served little purpose, aside from being a meeting place for Scandinavians staying at nearby hotels, and yet the sales department located there was unable to handle the phonecalls from customers and travel agents.

At the airport, meanwhile, the workload for employees was uneven. SAS had only one daily round-trip passenger connection, a flight between Stuttgart and Copenhagen. The plane landed in the evening and took off again in the morning. An SAS cargo plane also made a stopover in the morning. The cargo people in particular had very little to do for long stretches of time.

So Werner decided to consolidate all the employees and services at the airport location and closed the downtown office. At the same time he rearranged the organization. He had the passenger-service employees from the airport and the sales staff from downtown teach each other how to do their jobs. This reciprocal training program, intended to introduce new work routines, also broadened the employees' knowledge of the overall operation.

Today, a number of SAS functions in Stuttgart are integrated. The sales people are now responsible for both cargo and passenger sales. And everybody pitches in to answer phones, sell tickets, check in passengers, handle customer problems, and conduct load checks.

As a result of Werner's changes, the Stuttgart office now costs SAS less money both because one fewer office is open and because the employees' time is spent more productively. And, most importantly, no services were cut! In fact, service is probably *better* because the organization is more flexible. Now that everyone knows each other's jobs, there is always someone around who can handle the problems of the moment. And for many employees, work has become more fun and challenging.

The Stuttgart story shows that flattening the traditional organizational pyramid works. Any business organization seeking to establish a customer orientation and create a good impression during its "moments of truth" must flatten the pyramid—that is, eliminate the hierarchical tiers of responsibility in order to respond directly and quickly to customers' needs. The customer-oriented company is organized for change.

"Managing" is thus shifted from the executive suite to the operational level where everyone is now a manager of his own situation. When problems arise, each employee has the authority to analyze the situation, determine the appropriate action, and see to it that the action is carried out, either alone or with the help of others.

It may seem like a mere word game to call everyone a "manager," but I use the term to remind my staff—and perhaps most those at the upper levels of the old pyramid—that their roles have undergone a fundamental change. If the top executives who were once the managers must learn to be leaders, then those people out in the front lines must make all the operational decisions. They are the ones who most directly influence the customer's impression of the company during those "moments of truth."

Consider the following before-and-after scenario of how flattening the pyramids might make an airline staff better able to serve its passengers' needs.

Let's say that you've pre-ordered a special vegetarian meal for your SAS flight from Stockholm to New York. Nervously, you approach the check-in counter to find out whether your meal has been delivered to the plane.

"I don't know," the agent sighs. "I'm sorry, but I'm busy, and I'm not familiar with the food service."

"But what can I do?" you ask.

"You'll have to ask at the gate," she replies. "They'll certainly be able to help you there."

The agent quickly moves on to help the next person in line. Given no alternative, you go to the gate and ask again.

The gate attendant is friendly, but he doesn't know where your meal is either. "I wish I could help, but I don't have anything to do with food service. Just check with the stewardess when you get on board and things should certainly work out."

Reluctantly, you board the plane. When you ask the stewardess about your vegetarian meal, she is bewildered.

She hasn't heard anything about special food orders, but the plane is about to take off and nothing can be done now. "You should have contacted us earlier," she reprimands. "There would have been no problem if only we had known in time."

In this situation, the hierarchical organizational structure has caused the airline to ruin three "moments of truth." No one the passenger encountered had the authority to handle the specific problem, and no one dared step out of his normal role to try to solve it.

Let's now suppose that the organization has changed its structure by flattening the pyramid and putting a team of people in charge of the Stockholm-New York flight from start to finish.

The team has 15 members, two of whom function as "coaches," one indoors and one out by the plane. The indoor coach sits in on the flight crew's briefing and consults with them about pre-flight information such as the appropriate time to begin boarding, whether any infants or disabled people are on the passenger list, and whether anyone has ordered a special meal.

In the morning, the indoor team assembles at the check-in counters to solve passengers' ticketing problems, assign seats, handle fragile baggage, and so forth. When a mother arrives with her baby, she is greeted with a smile and told that a suspended cradle has already been put on board and that the seat beside hers will be kept free if at all possible.

When you arrive at check-in and ask about your vegetarian meal, you won't be hurriedly dismissed by the agent behind the counter. Thanks to the new team arrangement, your meal request becomes that agent's responsibility. She can confirm that it is already on board—or take steps to make sure it's loaded by the time you step into the plane.

As more and more passengers check in, the SAS team gradually moves to the departure gate, where they nod to their passengers in recognition. They are well acquainted with the flight to New York and can answer all the usual questions: how to transfer from JFK to La Guardia, why there is a stopover in Oslo, the actual flight time, and whether the captain will announce when they are flying over Greenland.

Problems are solved on the spot, as soon as they arise. No frontline employee has to wait for a supervisor's permission. No passenger boards the plane while still worried or dissatisfied.

Furthermore, by giving more responsibility to the frontline personnel, we are letting them provide the service that they had wanted to provide all along but couldn't because of an inflexible hierarchical structure.

Take, for example, the announcements made over a plane's public address system. In the old days, the SAS rule book included paragraphs that the crew read verbatim. When we gave the employees more flexibility, we encouraged them to toss out the script and improvise in a conversational matter that suited them, the passengers, and the current situation on the plane.

And did our employees take our advice? At least one of them certainly did. On the morning flight from Stockholm to Copenhagen on September 20, 1982—the day after the Social Democrats were returned to power after a six-year hiatus—the captain picked up the microphone and said, "Good morning, comrades." Then he went on to deliver a brilliant political satire.

Now, no instruction manual could have detailed how to address a plane full of businessmen on the morning after a Socialist victory. Allowed to take responsibility for the situation, however, the captain seized a "moment of truth" that the passengers aren't likely to forget.

On another flight, a curious coach passenger peeked into the first-class cabin. Catching his eye, the purser invited him in and showed him around. After a tour of the cockpit too, the purser offered him a drink. "How do you like working for SAS these days?" the passenger asked.

"It's wonderful—like being at an entirely new company."

"How, specifically?"

"Well, I can bring a passenger in here and offer him a drink without having to ask anybody's permission or write a report later accounting for my actions or the missing drinks."

Of course, the organizational transformation at SAS has not always been smooth and painless. In our hurry to find some quick solutions to SAS's financial problems when I first joined the company, we flattened the organizational structure so rapidly that we certainly stumbled occasionally along the way.

At first, so that the effects of our changes would be immediate, we simply circumvented middle managers and went directly to the front line. The front line, too, bypassed middle managers and came straight to the top for assistance. We responded by issuing company-wide memos reaffirming that the front line had the power to make individual decisions.

Initially we met with such fantastic success with the frontline people that we didn't notice anything was wrong elsewhere in the organization.

Yet, the middle managers, who were understandably confused by their new role within the organization, became hostile and counterproductive. We had put them in a completely unfamiliar situation where they were squeezed from both directions. Directives came shooting down from above that conflicted with their expectations and experience. They heard what we said but didn't know how to translate it into practical actions. From below came demands for reponsibility and power to make decisions, which they viewed as a threat to their own position.

We had directed middle managers to go out and listen to the people in the front line—to find out what they needed to do their jobs. The managers, however, were not accustomed to thinking of themselves as filling a support function, especially if they are supporting people previously considered subordinates. The word "support" conjures up an image of attending to needs, not administering. At SAS, like at other companies, support and service had always been relegated to a low status. Every promotion had moved people away from serving the customer and toward administration.

So, even after we reorganized the company, middle managers continued to sit in their offices lined with regulations books, policies, and directives. And when the people on the front lines "broke the rules" to help the customers, naturally the middle managers responded by reining them in. This infuriated the front line.

Although our new strategy of decentralizing responsibility was a big hit with our frontline employees, we had a much tougher time finding the right way to inspire middle managers. For example, upon returning from the United States to Sweden one time I entered the terminal and was met by a chaotic scene. Apparently the monitors matching up flight numbers with the corresponding conveyor belts that carried the baggage were on the blink, and everyone was madly searching for their luggage.

I suggested to the woman at the information counter that she post a few signs—handwritten, if need be—to alleviate the confusion.

"I wish I could," she responded. "The system broke down last Monday and I told the boss then that we should put up some temporary signs so people could find their baggage. But he said that it would be fixed soon enough, so the signs were unnecessary."

"But that was a week ago!"

"I know! But now that an entire week has gone by, he says the monitors are *sure* to be fixed soon."

Back at the head office I phoned the appropriate division head and asked him to give the woman's boss a choice: he could take his handsome desk from his spacious office and move it down to the arrivals terminal, where he could witness the problems personally and continue making decisions about them. Or he could stay right where he was. But if he did, he would have to yield his decision-making power to the frontline people in the arrivals terminal.

The supervisor had not understood that his role had changed under our new organization. In the past he had issued orders and instructions to his staff. Now his job was to serve them by ensuring that they understood their department's objectives and that they had the information and resources required to meet those objectives down in the arrivals terminal. He wasn't supposed to sit in his office and decide whether or not handwritten baggage signs should be posted.

Much of the fault for this was ours. We had let our middle managers down. We had given the front line the right to accept responsibility, yet we hadn't given middle managers viable alternatives to their old role as rule interpreters. We hadn't told middle management how to handle what might, at first glance, look like a demotion.

Let me give you another example of the initial mixed success of our organizational changes at SAS.

One day an SAS flight across Sweden had fallen far behind schedule because of snow. Taking responsibility for the situation, the purser decided on her own to compensate the customers for their inconvenience by offering free coffee and biscuits. She knew from experience that, because she was offering them at no charge, she would need about 40 additional servings. So she went to catering and ordered the extra coffee and biscuits.

The SAS catering supervisor turned her down. It was against regulations to request more than the amount of food allotted to a particular flight, and the supervisor refused to budge. But the purser wasn't thwarted. She noticed a Finnair plane docked at the next gate. Finnair is an external customer of the SAS catering department, and as such is not subject to SAS internal regulations.

Thinking quickly, the SAS purser turned to her colleague in the Finnair plane and asked him to order 40 cups of coffee and 40 biscuits. He placed the order which, according to regulations, the catering supervisor was obligated to fulfill. Then the SAS purser bought the snack from Finnair with SAS petty cash and served the grateful passengers.

In this case, the purser dared to find a way to circumvent regulations in order to meet the customers' needs—something she surely never would have tried under the old system. At the same time, however, the catering supervisor couldn't understand why a lowly purser had the right to make decisions that had always been in his purview and so he became confused and angry.

What he hadn't realized—what we hadn't adequately explained—was that he never should have questioned her authority or in any way have interfered with her attempt to satisfy customers. In that "moment of truth," the purser had to act quickly or forever lose an opportunity to satisfy those customers. She could have taken her request to her supervisor, but that action would have initiated a bureaucratic process that would have remained unresolved long after the late flight had finally departed. The catering supervisor could have questioned the purser's decision later, but no one has the authority to interfere during a moment of truth. Seizing these golden opportunities to serve the customer is the responsibility of the front line. Enabling them to do so is the responsibility of middle managers.

Eventually, we formed a much clearer idea of how the flattened pyramid should operate and were able to communicate the new roles to middle managers as well. The work still begins with something handed down from above—overall objectives for achieving the company goals. Upon receiving these broad objectives, middle management first breaks them down into a set of smaller objectives that the frontline people will be able to accomplish. At that point the role of middle manager is transformed from administration to support.

People sometimes equate delegating responsibility with abdicating one's own influence. But that's hardly the case. Actually, the middle manager's role is indispensable in the smooth functioning of a decentralized organization.

To motivate the front line and support their efforts requires skilled and knowledgeable middle managers who are proficient at coaching, informing, criticizing, praising, educating, and so forth. Their authority applies to translating the overall strategies into practical guidelines that the front line can follow and then mobilizing the necessary resources for the front line to achieve its objectives. This requires hard-nosed business planning along with healthy doses of creativity and resourcefulness.

For example, the middle manager might ask the ramp employees to unload the luggage from each flight onto the conveyor belts before the passengers arrive to pick it up. The frontliner responds: "Okay, I accept your challenge. I can get the luggage there ahead of the passengers. But to be able to do it, I need three new trucks and seven additional workers." In other words, he tells the middle manager, "If you want me to take on this objective, I'll do it. But you must give me the resources to achieve the goal." And it's up to the middle manager to find a way to do it.

If it's an acute problem, the middle manager should reallocate his budget accordingly. A creative and brave manager might even exceed his budget hoping that the better results would be coming in by the time he would be held accountable. A middle manager who has not understood our new organization would flatly deny the request since it hadn't been provided for in the budget.

The important point here is that managers should evaluate the extra expense in terms of the market segment that it would benefit. If the investment is consistent with the strategy of serving the business traveler's needs, it should be approved. And if not, the resources should be reserved for services that do accomplish that objective.

You can get people to develop their skills not by steering them with fixed rules but by giving them the total responsibility to achieve a specified result. Let me give you another example in detail.

The most important factor in a business traveler's choice of an airline is scheduling—flights must be frequent and convenient. The second most important factor is punctuality. Flights must depart on time.

When I came to SAS, the company's reputation for punctuality was quickly deteriorating. It was evident in the behavior of our passengers. Our planes were late so often that they had grown accustomed to getting to the airport at the last minute—or even later. If they arrived in plenty of time, they just had to wait for delayed departures. Even the staff had stopped hurrying.

There had been much talk about improving punctuality but no action; suggestions for improvement were usually rejected, the argument being that punctuality would require more personnel and more planes in reserve, and that would be too expensive.

We soon realized the real problem was that no one was taking full responsibility for punctuality. So we looked for an appropriate point in the organization to place that responsibility.

Our operations control center, located in Copenhagen, was already making sure the planes were where they were supposed to be, that the crews were called in, and so on. So we asked John Sylvest, the manager in charge of the center, if he was prepared to take responsibility for turning SAS into Europe's most punctual airline within six months. He accepted the task, and then we asked him to calculate how much it would cost.

He reported to our Stockholm office armed with detailed charts and documentation and assisted by knowledgeable experts, ready to defend his study point by point. We stopped him short and asked him to tell us just his conclusions. He answered, "$1.8 million, and six months to pull it off."

True, we were losing a lot of money at the time, but $1.8 million to become the most punctual airline in Europe within six months was peanuts. We gave him the go-ahead without even asking for his specific recommendations.

John was a bit baffled. Weren't we interested in all the facts and suggestions he had intended to show us? No. We were interested in the results. The means were entirely up to him.

Within only four months, we had achieved our goal—and at a cost of $200,000.

How did this happen?

Remember that airline travelers judge punctuality not by the time of arrival but by the time of departure. People get jittery as the minutes tick away and the plane still hasn't departed. And so it was SAS departure times that John Sylvest targeted for improvement.

The major pitfall turned out to be our heightened attention to service. Our employees were delaying takeoffs until connecting flights arrived, even if those flights were late. After all, it could not be considered very good service to leave passengers behind! As a result, too many SAS planes stayed on the ground while waiting for each other. This problem was compounded worldwide every day, and it only got worse.

But once we made a commitment to punctuality, the solution was simple: if a plane didn't arrive in time for its connections, then it was just too bad. The other planes weren't going to wait. By not compounding our delays, we made tremendous progress toward prompt departures.

If a flight attendant had not arrived by departure time, passengers had been forced to sit in the terminal and wait until a replacement was found. Now the control center issued new instructions: leave on time, as long as you don't fall below the minimum crew number. Safety was not to be compromised, but passengers probably were willing to accept a little slower cabin service in exchange for punctuality.

Similar policies applied to food. If the manual said there had to be one tray for every passenger and by a mistake the plane came up one tray short, the crew held the flight until the additional tray was brought aboard. But John Sylvest's plan changed that too. "Depart on time," he now told the staff. "There's always someone who has just eaten or someone going for dinner right after arrival. If all else fails, ask if SAS can buy them a meal when they arrive. It's worth the expense to stay on time."

Next, John Sylvest tackled another product-oriented practice called "consolidation." If a flight were only half full, it was sometimes cancelled and its passengers would be put on the next available plane. Consolidation was a frequent occurrence on the flights between Stockholm, Oslo, and Copenhagen in the interest of saving fuel during the energy crises.

Although the previous year SAS had saved $2.6 million by consolidating flights, the practice really frustrated the passengers and undermined punctuality. So John intended to use the $1.8 million to ensure that all scheduled flights ran, even if they were less than half full.

By the time his plan was to take effect, however, SAS's revitalized reputation for punctuality was attracting so many new customers that there were no longer any half-empty planes to consolidate!

The punctuality campaign's most important achievement was rallying everyone at SAS behind the same objective. Our former target had been that 80 percent of the planes would depart on time. This gave everybody an escape valve: 20 percent of the planes were allowed to be late, so what difference would it make if they didn't hurry to make sure *their* flight was on time?

Now the target was 100 percent. With no further directives from top management, everyone tried to work a little more smoothly and efficiently. Punctuality had become a group concern. Before, nobody was responsible. Now, everyone was.

The punctuality campaign received an unexpected boost by our introduction of a new position called "service manager." The service manager makes sure that problems are resolved on the ground and not passed on to the plane's crew. He also facilitates passenger boarding. If there is a tremendously large crowd, he overrides the manual's dictums about how many minutes before departure the passengers are to be allowed on the plane and starts boarding earlier.

The technical side of the company offered its own contributions. According to the maintenance guidelines, it should take 15 to 19 hours to check over a DC-9. But these times had gradually increased just as punctuality was slipping elsewhere in the company, so planes were not always available when they were needed. By tightening up service time, we were able to get planes out of the shop in 15 to 19 hours again. But our increased speed did not compromise safety. In fact, the punctuality drive stimulated a general increase in precision, which in turn heightened attention to safety.

My participation in the campaign came as a surprise—even to me! One day the door to my office opened and several people ushered in my new computer terminal. I hadn't requested any such thing—but it turned out the company's new director of the service division had ordered it for me. He felt that we should show the organization we were intent on following the progress of the punctuality drive by having the president personally keep track of every situation.

The terminal was automatically updated every five minutes. I could watch both the overall progress of our punctuality drive and specific cases of good and mediocre work. Seeing, for instance, that the Oslo people managed to get a flight off on time in spite of poor weather conditions, I immediately phoned them with a word of appreciation. Or if a flight was running behind, I could call the service manager and say, "This is Jan Carlzon. I was just wondering why that flight got off late."

Of course, in the long run, it isn't my job to monitor which flights depart on time and which are late. But during early phases of the campaign, it certainly showed every SAS employee how much we valued their attention to punctuality.

Despite some minor setbacks along the way, the SAS pyramid has truly been flattened, and our employees tell us that they're working with newfound motivation and confidence.

I urge others to take a close, hard look at their own organizations. If you can flatten your own pyramids you will be creating a far more powerful and resilient organization that not only serves customers better but also unleashes the hidden energy within your employees. The results can be absolutely astounding.

# 7

# TAKING RISKS

There is a popular Swedish tale about a medieval girl named Ronia, who befriends a neighbor boy even though their families have long been enemies. The two families live on opposite sides of a chasm so deep that anyone who tries to leap it and fails will fall to certain death.

Because the boy was Ronia's friend, he has come to visit her in her family's fortress. Upon seeing him, Ronia's father takes him prisoner, intending to use the young hostage to defeat the other family.

Ronia stands at the edge of the chasm and prepares to jump. If she can make it across to the other side, she reasons, she will be taken prisoner by the boy's family and the two sides will be even again. If she misses, all is lost. She will plummet to her death, and her friend will be at her father's mercy.

It will take all of her courage. If she misses, the consequences will be dire. Yet this is her only chance.

She jumps across!

Ronia knew that there are times when a person has to jump. Those who always choose the safest path will never

75

get across the chasm. They will be left standing on the wrong side.

Similarly, individual employees—and corporations as a whole—must dare to take the leap. In the corporate world, taking this kind of leap is called "execution." Having a clearly stated strategy makes the execution much easier. It is a matter of courage, sometimes bordering on foolhardiness, combined with a large portion of intuition. These characteristics may be impossible to acquire but, if possessed, can always be developed further.

The ideas behind what we did at Linjeflyg and SAS were neither new nor original. But we had the courage to act on them as no one else had. By cutting fares at Linjeflyg, we transformed Sweden's domestic air travel industry from a service almost exclusively for businessmen into one that everyone was talking about and eager to use. Literally hundreds of people have since told me, "There was nothing new about that. We've been saying for years that you should lower prices. It's obvious that you could attract more passengers if you cut prices in half."

Sure, the idea was simple and obvious. In fact, several airlines had considered cutting prices at the time, but their calculations led them to conclude that the risks were too great. I am quite certain that if I had been a more cautious and prudent person, I would have failed completely at Linjeflyg. I too would have done my calculations, route by route, until the magnitude of the risk became so enormous that I would have rejected the notion altogether. But instead I dared to rely more on my intuition than on my pocket calculator. Cutting prices at Linjeflyg was my own Ronia's chasm.

The same was true in the case of SAS. We could not measure or calculate our way to knowing whether our proposed changes and marketing investments would bring in enough new revenue. Beyond rough economic estimates, we had only our intuition for guidance. But once we dared to take the leap, we gained much more than we ever could have imagined.

Unfortunately, many corporate executives are noticeably lacking in intuition, courage, and conviction. The hierarchical company is traditionally headed by people highly skilled in economics, finance, or other technical expertise. These people may be extremely bright, but they are often disastrous decision-makers and implementers. They find 10 solutions to every problem, and just as they are about to decide which one to try, they discover five more. In the meantime, opportunities have passed them by. They are faced with entirely new problems and must start the process all over again. Sometimes I suspect they think up new alternatives in order to avoid taking the crucial leap.

Now, I do not oppose analytical thinking. Analysis is crucial, but it must be directed toward the overall business strategy, not toward the individual elements of that strategy. To the rational observer, investing an additional $50 million in improvements at a time when SAS was losing $20 million a year might have appeared reckless. Indeed, it would have been just that had the improvements not been integrated into an overall business strategy.

Before concluding that we needed to make those investments, we analyzed the business environment, formulated an objective, and developed a strategy. Only after we had established a logical context did I take the leap. Once again, like Ronia, I realized that jumping involved a huge risk—but at the same time it was our only chance.

To succeed in executing an idea that no one else has dared to try, you usually have to take a *big* leap. Linjeflyg had tried price cuts earlier—but so sheepishly that the market didn't catch on. Several airlines had launched a business class before SAS did, but they had not made a real dent in the market. Taking small steps, like offering free drinks, won't be enough when you're peering over the edge of a chasm.

The issue of timing must also be considered in your business analysis. Do you remember who launched turbo-charged engines in cars? Most people would probably guess Saab. Few would recall that BMW introduced its turbo as early as 1974. Why? Because BMW's timing was the worst imaginable: the turbo was launched in the middle of the oil crisis, when conservation measures made people more interested than ever before in high-mileage cars and slower driving.

Part of the reason many business executives won't leap the chasm is that they assume most things can't be done. Top management at SAS, for example, habitually calculated the odds of obtaining government permission to make a change. Usually determining that the response would be no, they rarely actually submitted a proposal. Instead, they routinely killed good ideas early in their development with arguments such as "the authorities will never let us" or "that will never work."

I have a saying that helps shake off psychological obstacles like these: "Run through walls." Your goal may seem impossible, but don't stop trying to accomplish it until someone really says no. The walls towering before you may not be as massive as they appear. Maybe they're not stone walls at all but cardboard facades that you can run straight through.

One of the first times I ran through a wall, I did so inadvertently. While president of Vingresor, I heard that Thomson, a major British travel firm, earned $20 per head over and above the money they made on the tour package itself—profits from selling T-shirts, excursions, and so forth. At Vingresor we made less than one-tenth that amount.

With our clientele of 200,000 passengers a year, it was obvious that there were millions of dollars to be made.

I explained the situation to Claes Bernhard, one of our marketing people, and charged him with equalling Thomson's success. "Do it whatever way you like," I instructed, "but our minimum target is $20 per customer." Claes launched fantastic promotional gimmicks and arranged in-company sales contests, giving the staff a chance to win everything from cars to cows. Our profit finally crept up to $8 per head but then plateaued. Disappointed and perplexed, I sent Claes to Thomson to find out how they managed to do it.

The people at Thomson were astonished. It turned out that I had misinterpreted the figures. They made $20 per head, all right, but that was their *gross* revenue. Their net profit was actually less than ours had been all along. Now, had I known that from the start, I probably would have been satisfied with the status quo. My misunderstanding, however, inspired me to run through a wall and increase Vingresor's profits substantially.

At Linjeflyg we ran up against another seemingly insurmountable wall. In the five years before I arrived, the company had purchased 13 jets, putting it $70 million in debt. It wasn't the debt itself that bothered me as much as the fact that we had bought the jets from Fokker in the Netherlands, and so we owed the money in Dutch florins rather than Swedish kronor. The exchange rate was brutal; in fact, currency fluctuations alone had accounted for $10 to $12 million of the debt. Moreover, because we were so heavily in debt, we were having trouble securing a bank loan to pay off the purchase. The situation had to change.

I made our new administrative manager, Bengt Hagglund, responsible for repatriating the loans from the Dutch to the Swedish market. Then I watched him run right through all the walls. Bengt contacted every credit institution in Sweden about borrowing money. And despite Linjeflyg's poor debt-equity ratio, they came through. The banks believed in our new strategy and in the security that goes with a public utility. Bengt handled the job expertly on his own—much better, that is, than if I had gone the traditional route and told him exactly what to do. That would only have stifled his creativity, which proved to be considerable.

After we reorganized SAS and unleashed our employees' energy, our people began to break through walls routinely. When we were about to inaugurate EuroClass, for instance, we wanted to enhance the product we offered our business travelers. One facet was separate and faster check-in counters. Common wisdom held that the authorities in egalitarian Scandinavia would never approve because it would create an unequal separation of social classes. A typical wall. But what happened? We submitted our request anyway and explained our overall strategy. The Scandinavian boards of civil aviation understood our request as an important component of our turnaround strategy and approved it immediately.

The biggest wall we faced—and still ran through—was the one that appeared when we tried to launch EuroClass in the face of strong opposition from other European airlines. The previous year, Air France had instituted a similar business class system. But their Classe Affaires was available only to those passengers who paid a surcharge over the normal full-fare coach price.

When we introduced SAS EuroClass, our aim was to provide better service to those who had already paid the relatively high cost of a full-fare coach ticket. Air France, however, expected us to collect a similar surcharge.

We refused. We once would have acquiesced to our competitors' demands. At the new SAS, however, we realized that we couldn't abandon our business strategy even if our determination touched off a war between civil aviation authorities, which is exactly what happened.

Air France, however, had leverage over us. Commercial aviation in Europe is regulated by a series of bilateral civil aviation agreements among the various countries. In trying to establish a measure of equality regarding production volume, pricing, and levels of service, these agreements, in essence, give each country's airlines veto power over the others' actions. Furthermore, Air France is wholly owned by the French government.

Though it seems extreme for France to terminate its airline agreements with Scandinavia just because SAS refused to charge passengers more money for better service, that was the situation in 1981. The French authorities threatened to stop SAS from flying to France. SAS hasn't always agreed with its governments, but this time we received superb backing; the Scandinavian authorities responded with a parallel threat against Air France.

That put Air France in something of a fix. Whereas using moveable partitions allowed us to adjust the size of the EuroClass section to accommodate the number of Euro-Class and discount passengers traveling on each flight, Air France had built permanent Classe Affaires sections on their planes. Thus, their Classe Affaires passenger capacity—and, by extension, their profitability—was physically restricted.

We stuck to our guns, but so did Air France, which received the support of at least some of the other commercial carriers in Europe. We were fighting almost the entire European airline industry. It was clearly the most massive wall that had ever loomed before us. We had no choice but to run right through it.

In an effort to keep Classe Affaires competitive with EuroClass, Air France lowered its business fares to match ours and slashed full-fare coach prices even more. We retaliated by lowering our normal fares. A bilateral price war ensued and continued to wage until both the French and Swedish foreign ministers met in Stockholm, with the two airlines in the background, to resolve the conflict. They agreed that SAS could continue to offer EuroClass without a surcharge. Air France, in turn, would be allowed to charge our price in their Classe Affaires and could give slight discounts to those normal-fare passengers who could not be seated in the business class section. (Air France never implemented this system, and to this day they have trouble with their price structure and Classe Affaires seating capacity on their Scandinavian flights.)

Why was this issue so important to us? Because if we had been forced to charge extra on EuroClass flights to France, the whole strategy behind EuroClass would have collapsed. By running through the Air France wall, we established once and for all the principle that EuroClass would cost no more than the full-fare coach. By backing up our commitment to execute our business strategy, we were able to achieve our goal.

Without a clearly enunciated strategy, we never would have received unquestioning support from the Scandinavian authorities. The Air France battle was also a fantastic morale-booster for our employees. Everyone united in the fight against an external enemy to uphold a principle we all shared.

Not only must those in top management learn to leap the chasm, but risk-taking must ripple throughout the *entire* organization.

Unfortunately, most frontline employees have been following regulations for so long that few have the courage to try something unusual. Instead of making a decision that a superior might dislike, they will delegate responsibility back up—in the most extreme cases, all the way to the board of directors. (This happens more often than most corporate executives would care to admit.)

If frontline employees are actually to make decisions that entail some risk, they must have a sense of security. Having knowledge and information is not enough if they believe that a wrong decision may cause them problems or even the loss of their job. They must know that they are allowed to make mistakes. Only then will they dare to use fully their new authority.

Such security comes from two sources: internal and external. Top and middle managers can nurture both.

Internal security can arise from a heightened sense of self-worth that greater responsibility engenders. As Eric Fromm points out, no person can "own" power and authority in its traditional meaning because the day he loses the fancy title and the big office he also loses his authority. In reality, authority and responsibility are linked to the individual—to his wisdom, knowledge, and way of dealing with people. This gives him an authority no one can take away. Ideally, then, frontline employees should draw their sense of security from within.

External security must be assured by those in the higher organizational levels. Leaders and managers must give guidance, not punishment, to employees who take risks and, occasionally, make mistakes. Wrong decisions should be used as the basis for training; right decisions should be used as the basis for praise and positive examples. A person who is admonished for his mistakes should be entitled to appeal his case without fear of retribution.

I should clarify here that the right to make mistakes is not equivalent to the right to be incompetent, especially not as a manager. A manager cannot be allowed to keep his position if he does not accept his company's overall strategy or if he is incapable of meeting his objectives.

Sweden's "Aman" laws, which guarantee that an employee cannot be fired without good cause, have compelled us to take a hard look at employment security. Perhaps many U.S. business executives would take issue with this legislation, but I think it's a blessing. It provides a basic platform of security that allows the decentralization of responsibility and encourages some risk-taking.

Surprisingly, in decentralizing SAS, we have met with less success in the United States than anywhere else. We like to think of America as the land of the free and the home of the brave, but Americans are actually reluctant to take risks in their daily jobs. I think this is because most U.S. companies do not offer real job security. Either you keep the boss happy or you don't get paid next week.

Another example, one that harkens back to our punctuality campaign at SAS, further illustrates my point about encouraging all levels of employees to take risks.

One time an important executive of Swedish business radioed ahead from his business jet as he was approaching Kennedy Airport to let SAS know he would be a few minutes late for the flight to Stockholm. Though he didn't actually say it, the clear implication was that we should hold the plane.

Once, we would have done just that. No one would even consider leaving such an important person behind and risk such influential ill-will. There were no standing instructions, but it would not have been wise to leave without that VIP. It would have been safer to wait than risk a strong reprimand.

But when he arrived, the plane had already departed on time. An SAS official greeted him and explained that he was booked on a KLM flight leaving half an hour later. It would be the same type of aircraft and the executive would be assigned the same seat number he always booked on SAS. He had no complaint, and SAS had maintained its reputation for punctuality—all because one employee had dared to find an unusual solution to the problem.

On another occasion I was sitting with the pilots up in the cockpit when it was time to leave. The seconds ticked away down to the magic moment. Would we take off on time? Then the captain muttered something about a light indicating a fault somewhere on board. A door wasn't properly closed. Grabbing the microphone, he asked the cabin crew to open and close that door once again. While they were at the door, the second hand on the clock ticked past the departure time. Suddenly we felt a thud in the plane. *What* was that? The captain broke out into a wide grin and pointed downward. It was the driver of the pushback truck who, in all friendliness, was signaling that it was time to go!

This incident may seem insignificant to an outsider, but for me, aware of the once-enormous difference in status between a truck driver and a captain at SAS, it was a very telling experience. It was hard proof that we were all pulling together in our campaign to make SAS the most punctual airline in the world.

And since then SAS has been Europe's most punctual airline.

# 8

## COMMUNICATING

In 1981, as we were preparing to implement many organizational changes at SAS, we distributed to all 20,000 employees a red-covered booklet called "Let's Get in There and Fight, soon popularly nicknamed "the little red book." The booklet was a tool to help us present our overall vision and strategy and, more specifically, our expectations of the employees themselves.

Many people thought the little red book was far too simplistic for SAS's many intellectual and highly educated employees. It had only a few words, in big type, on each page and was filled with cartoonlike drawings of an airplane smiling, frowning, and even covering its eyes with its wings as it went into a nosedive.

Simplistic or not, the little red book was an effective communications tool internally. Having done away with the old hierarchical structure, we couldn't *order* our employees to do things differently. Instead, we had to convey our vision of the company and *convince* them that they could and should take responsibility for carrying out that vision. The little red book's pictures and words did just that.

Many of the stories I have already told about how we motivated our employees and unleashed hidden energy within the company are really stories about informing, persuading, and inspiring—in a word, communicating. In a decentralized, customer-driven company, a good leader spends more time communicating than doing anything else. He must communicate with the employees to keep them all working toward the same goals, and he must communicate with his customers to keep them abreast of the company's new activities and services.

From my first day at SAS I've made communicating, particularly with our employees, a top priority. In fact, during the first year I spent exactly half of my working hours "out in the field" talking to SAS people. The word going around was that any time three employees gathered, Jan Carlzon would probably show up and begin talking with them. It was my way of accepting responsibility and showing that my enthusiasm and involvement were genuine.

In a hierarchical company where the boss issues orders, it is up to the employees to understand what these orders mean. The boss need only make sure that he words the message correctly. But in a company like SAS, a leader communicating a strategy to thousands of decentralized decision-makers who must then apply that general strategy to specific situations must go much further. Rather than merely issuing your message, you have to be certain that every employee has truly understood and absorbed it. This means you have to reverse the approach: you must consider the words that the receiver can best absorb and make them your own.

This may well compel business leaders to use plainer, more straightforward language. But there is no such thing as an "oversimplified" phrase. It is better to be too clear or too simple than to risk the possibility that one of your employees will misunderstand your message. The little red book was a classic example.

Clear and simple messages issued from a leader help establish targets that everyone can work toward. When John F. Kennedy declared, "I want a man on the moon before 1970," for example, he set up a target for an entire nation. He wasn't the one who was going to do the actual work, but his vital contribution was this single, brief statement. It steered scientists' efforts in the same direction.

When Hakon Sundin was named the new coach of the Swedish national bandy team (bandy is similar to field hockey on ice) four years ago, his first statement to the press was: "We are going to be world champions in three years." That bold announcement followed a string of humiliating losses to the Russians, who were the reigning and perennial world champions. Everyone was convinced that the Russians would always be first and Sweden should regard second place as a victory. Sundin initiated a complete reversal by saying what he did. Even though no one believed him, Sweden did win a world championship three years later.

The most powerful messages are those that are simple and direct and can serve as a battle cry of sorts for people across all organizational levels. The message does not need to be lofty or even original.

After a speech people often tell me, "That was a phenomenal way of getting across obvious points." I'm not always certain whether they mean it as a compliment; maybe they're not certain either. But I believe I have successfully conveyed my message if what I said has come across as obvious. It means I have found a way to express something that strikes a resonant chord inside the people who are listening to me. I have reached them.

It was this ability to communicate that greatly helped me during my early days at Linjeflyg and SAS. By listening to the employees and speaking in simple terms, I was able to articulate their own thoughts. Not only did their input shape my strategic thinking, but the approach I've described here helped me win their support and, thus, helped the company achieve its goals.

There is no question that the kind of leadership communication I am calling for involves more than a little showmanship. If you want to be an effective leader, you cannot be shy or reticent. Knowing how to appear before large audiences and persuade them to "buy" your message is a crucial attribute of leadership—almost as crucial as being able to calculate or plan.

I have been told that I come across well on television, but I know it isn't because my ideas are necessarily unique; rather, it is because I've avoided cluttering them with words that the audience may not understand. My goal is to persuade people, not to show them that I know more than everyone else.

Take, for example, the public debate on the issue of income taxes during the 1979 Swedish election campaign. After 40 years of socialist rule, the top income tax rate in Sweden had soared to about 90 percent. Like many others, I argued that the government would realize *more* revenue from taxes if the marginal tax rate were lowered to 50 percent—sort of a Swedish version of the "Laffer curve." Determined to change some minds, I had to find a way to make people listen to the arguments in a new way.

I calculated that the marginal taxes above 50 percent brought the government $1.5 billion. So I went on television and said, "I'm willing to lock away $1.5 billion in a safe deposit box and hand over the keys to our political leaders. If they do as I say and cut the marginal tax rate Sweden will be better off—and then I want my $1.5 billion back and I'll want some influence over financial policies in the future. If I'm wrong, they can have my money and the country still won't have lost any revenue."

People accused me of using a gimmick, and, in a way, they were right. I certainly didn't have an extra $1.5 billion to give the Swedish government. But by delivering my message the way I did, it hit home. The story appeared in newspapers all over the world. From a small town in Florida, a certain "Colonel Faithful" sent me a letter thanking me for my suggestion. "Young man," he wrote, "even if that really was your last $1.5 billion, then you've certainly bet it on the right horse." Even across the Atlantic, I had struck a chord— as much because of the presentation as because of the idea itself.

Showmanship demands that you sometimes turn yourself inside out a little to communicate the message. The entertainer who fails to give something of himself will never reach the audience no matter how polished the performance. The same applies to the leader of a company.

Only once did I deliver a speech using a prepared manuscript. It was a complete disaster. There was nothing wrong with the content—it was a well-conceived, beautifully worded message. But I was no good at reading speeches.

Conversely, I have given hundreds of talks and lectures relying on no written words—just my own conviction. This allows me to expand a little, talk about something that just happened, or instantly adapt my words to the situation at hand. In Chapter 2 I described the day that I outlined the new business strategy to the employees of Linjeflyg. I had prepared a staid and sober speech about how life in Sweden had changed and how Linjeflyg must also change, but I quickly saw that the atmosphere was far too festive to recite that speech. I had to think on my feet in order to adapt to the excitement of the moment.

The same principles apply to communication outside the company through advertising, public relations, and general "image making." Unless you can communicate your business strategy clearly to your customers, you might as well not have developed it at all. Remember SAS's "Y50" fare—a remarkable 50 percent off the price of standby tickets for young people? Nobody knew what it meant. But everybody knew what Linjeflyg's "Hundred Note" meant. In that case, it wasn't the idea that attracted hundreds of thousands of customers as much as it was the way that the message was communicated.

When we began reorganizing SAS, our critics scoffed at our efforts as mere "promotional gimmicks." They claimed we had become too marketing oriented, but in fact we hadn't increased our marketing budget one cent. Rather, we were spending our money more effectively on messages that were easily understood.

Previously, our ads had been vague and generic, with proclamations like "Give the Swedes the World." Few people remember such an ad, and fewer still grasp its intended meaning. So when we introduced EuroClass, we announced "No need to stand in line!"; "New lounges for business travelers!"; "You don't have to fight for a good seat!"; and "As close as you can get to first class on a coach-class ticket!" Far from hype, this was solid information that air travelers could use in selecting an airline.

Communication involves more than just words and advertising images. It also includes symbols. Everything about a leader has symbolic value, from lifestyle and dress to behavior. I recall an example from Linjeflyg, which had the most boring office space imaginable. The president, however, had not only a large, bright office facing the street but also an executive dining room with seating for eight people. Anyone who ate there enjoyed tremendous prestige.

I realized immediately that the executive dining room had to go. Linjeflyg, a small company, was sending out the wrong signals by having such a pretentious dining room. If I began eating there myself, my actions would tacitly condone an image I didn't like. So for the first few weeks I left the building at lunchtime and bought a hot dog.

I was still looking for the right opportunity to close the dining room when one of my managers said we should be in better touch with our employees.

"Excellent!" I responded. "Let's start by eating lunch with everybody else. We'll do away with the executive dining room!" Without losing any time, we moved my desk into the dining room and converted my former office into a company conference room that anyone could use—something we really needed.

Meanwhile, the executives began eating their lunch in the staff canteen. It was an unmistakable sign that we were all at Linjeflyg to work together—not so that some of us could occupy large offices. Everyone heard the message loud and clear that something new was happening—that from now on it was results that counted and not prestige.

A leader's ways are watched carefully and adopted by others in the organization. Through their behavior in turn, the leader's personality starts to permeate the entire company.

All company managements gripe about the bad habits of their staff members. If they were to take a closer look at the patterns, however, they would see that this poor behavior usually originates at the top. Recently we at SAS management became concerned about the tremendous amount of business travel going on in the company. Entire groups were even beginning to travel to other cities just to discuss a few procedural details! What we had not realized at first was that eight members of top management had recently decided to spend a week touring the Soviet Union, a trip only marginally related to SAS business. I intervened and called off their trip, of course, but it was too late to stop the talk that had already spread throughout the company: "If they can do it, so can we!"

Leaders should be aware of how far non-verbal communication can go in illustrating the style that others in the organization should follow. And, in so doing, the leader will be helping create the very image that the organization presents to its customers.

When I first came to Linjeflyg, I traveled around to various airports. Toward the end of one of these visits, I sensed some uneasiness among the staff but didn't know why. Then one employee tactfully pointed out that they were waiting for me to board the plane.

"Is it ready?" I asked. "I didn't hear any announcement."

"No, but if you get on now and decide where you want to sit, we can board the rest of the passengers."

If you indicate by your actions that you are superior even to your customers, then you can hardly call yourself market oriented. I had just come from the intensely competitive tourist charter business where it was out of the question to take precedence over a passenger. So I waited until everyone else got on board and was happy there was an extra seat for me.

At SAS we pass out magazines and newspapers on the aircraft. We do not always have enough for everyone and sometimes the staff tries to be kind by offering me my pick first. "Out of the question," I tell them. "I cannot take any myself until I know that all the passengers have gotten what they want!"

I have heard more than once that the cabin crew interprets these tiny, symbolic gestures in this way: "Even top management is helping give the passengers good service. That shows respect for *our* jobs." By demonstrating that we ourselves come last after the customers, we are telling our employees—and the customers—what the ranking order really is.

Setting a good example is truly the most effective means of communication—and setting a poor one is disastrous! Most traditional managers drape themselves in imperial trappings. But when the customer comes first, you simply can't afford to do that.

# 9

# BOARDS AND UNIONS

When we decided to make SAS more service oriented, the pursers grumbled that they could give much better service if we gave them new food and beverage carts for the planes.

Obviously, having new carts would save many valuable minutes serving customers, particularly on short flights. But replacing the worn-out carts carried a price tag of $2 million. Who would approve $2 million for something as trivial as new carts when the airline was losing $20 million a year?

The question of whether to purchase new carts had been bouncing around the company for five years before I joined SAS, during which both management and the board evaded making a final decision. How could they calculate profitability on the investment if they were unaware of how the carts fit into the big strategic picture?

However, once our new customer-driven strategy was in place—with the board's enthusiastic approval—it was obvious to us that new carts were in fact an important part of that strategy. And because the directors had already approved our overall business strategy, we didn't need to approach them on this element of it. We authorized the $2 million expenditure ourselves.

I have said much in this book about communicating the big picture to middle management and frontline employees; it is one of the tools they need to do their jobs well in a decentralized business environment. Other groups within the company also must understand the overall strategy in order to contribute. Management often regards unions as an enemy and the board of directors as, at best, the final place to pass the buck. Both are, in fact, valuable resources that *must* be tapped to achieve the high-energy, customer-driven business goals such as those we set at SAS.

Remarkably, the typical management team doesn't share the overall business strategy with the board of directors. Many company presidents actually fear their boards. One chairman whom I know tries to keep the president off balance by beginning each board meeting with the same question: "Shall we fire the president?"

Company presidents who are intimidated by their boards keep their corporate visions to themselves and, instead, dole out to the board tidbits of information intended to make the management team look successful. At the same time, they "delegate upward," asking the board to approve even minor decisions. They then shuffle back to the organization and announce what the board decided. The decision becomes law because there is no higher authority to whom an appeal can be made. These laws are sent down into the whole organization and out to the front line for implementation.

Not only does this waste time and stifle the staff's motivation, but it is a poor way of utilizing the board's collective business experience. A board that is uninformed of the larger strategy will find it difficult to assess and appreciate the rationale behind management's requests.

If you ask the board to participate in determining the company's vision, however, you are beginning to use the board wisely. This allows the board to focus on overarching strategic issues rather than diffuse its efforts on details better addressed elsewhere in the company.

Habits being what they are, it is possible that the board will feel bypassed if it isn't involved in all decisions. This is not an easy situation! If top management has resolved to pass decisions, responsibility, and authority on to other parts of the organization, yet the board insists on being involved in making decisions about the details, then the entire system is thrown out of whack! Admittedly, it's tough striking a perfect balance between the board, senior management, and the organization.

Nonetheless, by freeing the board of minor decisions and the paperwork that accompanies them, the president can enlist the board members as sparring partners in strategically crucial matters and capitalize on the potential that their vast business experience holds for the company.

If I had gone to the Linjeflyg board in 1978 with a typical proposal to cut fares, the board would have demanded an intricate set of calculations to substantiate the plan. Instead, I presented the fare cut as part of a much larger concept—including increases in flight frequency, advertising, and promotion—and they accepted it on the basis of the same intuitive feelings that had prompted me to make the request. "Go with it!" they affirmed in unison.

At SAS, the board's support for the overall vision was utterly critical. The route we were taking involved making substantial investments in the midst of an unprofitable year for SAS during a general market slump. To their credit, the board members—led by Haldor Topsoe, our Danish chairman—understood our overall goal of turning the company around without depending on market growth to do it. Topsoe actually pitched in to help explain our plan—and without demanding a plethora of detailed calculations and investigations. I was extremely excited when the moment arrived to present the entire plan of operations to the board. "Moment" is perhaps the wrong word—it turned into a monologue that went on for several hours!

Seeing the big picture, the board accepted our plan without reservation. Achieve the goal, they directed; how you do it is up to you. What the board gave us as our guideline was, to put it bluntly, "Turn around the downhill slide and make us profitable. But *don't count* on market growth to do it!"

The fact is, right up until about this period the market had grown steadily for years and everyone was accustomed to stable, almost automatic profitability. But now growth had ground to a halt, and virtually everyone in the business was losing money. The assignment was to turn the company around—that was our overall goal. The way we did so was pretty much up to us. They managed to pave the way for change, focus on a new strategic direction, and leave the details to us—even though the details were going to cost about $50 million.

I frequently consult with the three SAS board chairmen privately—again, not to run every detail past them but to double-check that I am keeping SAS on the right course. Each of the chairmen is a leading Scandinavian businessman: one is a Norwegian banker, another a Swedish industrialist, and the other a Danish engineer and entrepreneur. Their collective expertise is a superb resource, and I regularly use them as a sounding board before approaching the board as a whole.

The union is another thorn in the side of many business leaders. But unions, too, have the potential for making a crucial contribution to the corporate effort.

In the hierarchical company, the unions represent the people at the bottom of the pyramid who receive orders and directives. Therefore, it is the unions' function to examine and question, on behalf of the workers, decisions that the company management has already made. The unions then serve as a brake on the management process.

But if you decentralize the decision-making process, then the role of the unions changes fundamentally. With their own rank and file now making decisions as an ongoing part of their new role, unions can no longer oppose those decisions. You cannot be an adversary to the very people whose interests you represent. Instead, unions must become *partners* with their members and with management.

In a company such as SAS, which has decentralized its decision-making, the union now has three roles.

First, and most important, is the cooperative role. Together with top management the unions participate in analyzing, discussing, and establishing the company's overall direction and strategy. The unions should participate with middle management in planning the acquisition and distribution of resources, determining the earning targets, devising investment guidelines, and so on. With the front line the unions play a natural part in backing up the people they represent, meaning those who now make all the decisions.

The second role of the unions is similar to that of an internal auditor. They should critically examine how well the company is complying with labor laws and collective agreements.

The third role is more traditional: unions still must sit down at the other side of the table during negotiations. But now that the unions have helped shape the company's operations and investments, they can no longer pursue an adversarial role that undermines the company's overall strategy. To do so would serve no purpose since they have been participating in the construction of the company's strategic foundation all along.

Unions that accept these roles become vital contributors, not threats, to the management process. Because of their relationship with the rank and file, unions have access to a large fund of knowledge, ideas, and opinions that might otherwise be unavailable to top management. Unions have a network of contacts out in the company that management lacks.

Coming from a business leader, these ideas may seem heretical. But I believe that social trends will soon compel unions and management to redefine their relationship and shed their traditionally adversarial roles. I don't mean that unions should assume the burden of pushing through developments in this direction. First, preconditions in society must change. Only after companies have adapted their goals, organizational structures, and procedures to the new social order can unions begin to adjust their own operations. At that point, there is no doubt that unions will influence companies and companies, in turn, will influence society.

Conditions in our society have already begun to change. In the 1960s the unions and Social Democrats pushed through some fundamental legislative changes that led to the passage in 1977 of Sweden's Act on Employee Participation in Decision Making—also known as the Co-Determination Act or by its Swedish acronym MBL. MBL requires companies to provide more information to employees and to consult with the unions on any major changes in the business. The passage of these laws confirmed that social attitudes were changing.

Although MBL had brought us closer to a horizontal society, the companies had not kept up with the changes and did not understand how to adjust to the new environment. Most executives reacted negatively and argued: "It will be too inefficient with MBL. Everything will take too much time." The MBL laws arrived before the change in attitudes had penetrated the companies. To apply MBL in the old organizational structure was as futile as trying to repair a medieval castle with adhesive tape. The role of the unions, meanwhile, was strengthened, as was the centralized structure of the entire union movement.

When we decided SAS should be more decentralized, however, we made the Co-Determination Act work to our advantage. We created the Airline Council, through which the labor unions take part in discussions of strategic management issues. We also have divisional councils, where union representatives participate in each division's resource planning. We do not have a formal structure for union participation on the front line, but we assume that unions support their members who do this work, and we are trying to help the unions adjust their structure to that of our own company.

We know that the unions are carefully observing the changes at SAS. Since our new organization enables us to "hot-wire" the system and interact directly with the front line, the unions are recognizing the need to flatten their own hierarchies so they can act more quickly and keep apace. Otherwise, they risk being no more than a rubber stamp for our decisions.

To expand the cooperative efforts, however, management must also learn to regard the unions as natural partners and genuine resources. Both parties must become familiar with each other's ways of thinking. We in management need to give the unions a chance to understand our reasoning processes.

It is true that the presence of union representatives might inhibit freewheeling and open discussion. And at first, our managers did behave differently at meetings where the unions were represented. Over time, however, that changed. "You needn't worry about that," one union representative told me when we were discussing the problem. "We've realized that you're human too."

If managers have a hard time adjusting to the new situation, it is by no means easier for the union officials. The adversarial dynamic has deep roots. To many elected union officials, distrust of management and its ideas seems natural and warranted. Thus, when management invites the unions to help develop the company's strategy, it is understandable that the union representatives are skeptical of their motives.

At SAS we still have not completely convinced the union representatives that their new role is both more attractive and more powerful than the old one. But we continue to point out the ineffectuality of their reacting only to minor decisions that top management has already made. If they instead agree to share responsibility for the major strategic decisions and planning, then they can be quite certain that the other decisions will also be more to their liking.

Early and frequent involvement is important in working with both the unions and the board. If they understand and embrace the company's overall vision, not only will management's relations with them be more cooperative but their participation and contributions will become truly invaluable to the new organization. Rather than getting derailed by isolated decisions or single activities, they will be able to view the big picture and assume even greater responsibility.

Indeed, I believe that the only way *any* group or individual can take responsibility is to understand the overall situation. I routinely share the knowledge that I have about where the company is and where it should be heading with the board, unions, and employees. For the vision to become a reality, it must be *their* vision too.

# 10

## MEASURING RESULTS

**W**hen I took over at SAS, one of the areas we began to reassess was our air cargo operation. For maximum efficiency and profitability, commercial airlines try to fill the "empty bellies" of passenger planes with air cargo. So the SAS cargo division had always measured its performance by the amount of freight carried, or how well they filled up the planes' bellies.

We soon realized that we had been measuring the wrong thing—an "executive suite" goal that had nothing to do with the needs of our cargo customers. Indeed, our cargo customers were more concerned about *precision*, or prompt deliveries to the specified locations. So we revised our strategy and established a new goal: to become the airline with the highest precision.

We thought we were doing very well on precision; our cargo people reported that only a small percentage of shipments did not arrive at their destination on time. But we decided to try a test anyway. We sent 100 packages to various addresses throughout Europe. The results were devastating. The small parcels were supposed to arrive the next day; however, the average was four days later. Our precision was terrible.

We had caught ourselves in one of the most basic mistakes a service-oriented business can make: promising one thing and measuring another. In this case, we were promising prompt and precise cargo delivery, yet we were measuring volume and whether the paperwork and packages got separated en route. In fact, a shipment could arrive four days later than promised *without* being recorded as delayed. Clearly, we needed to start measuring our success in terms of our promises.

This was more crucial than ever because of the way we had reorganized SAS. A decentralized company is much more in need of good measurement methods than is a hierarchical, centralized organization.

In the old method of working, standards originated at the top and filtered down through the organization, usually via written memos and middle managers. It was the employees' job to follow the standards. Of course, if the standards were ambiguous, they produced uneven results. An ambitious engineering manager might allow costs to skyrocket in pursuit of quality, while a more cautious colleague might opt for "adequacy" in order to keep a tight rein on costs.

But in a decentralized organization, employees at all levels must understand exactly what the target is and how best to achieve it. Once the frontline personnel—with the support of middle management—have taken on the responsibility of making specific decisions, these employees must have an accurate feedback system for determining whether the decisions they are making are, in fact, the ones that will accomplish the company's overall goals. In a customer-driven company, measurements are derived from how well they are focusing their energy on the areas that are vital to the paying customers.

The necessity of measuring results is particularly crucial for those employees who affect customer service through their work but who don't have face-to-face contact with those customers. Ticket agents get immediate feedback on their job performance hundreds of times a day from the customers they serve. However, other workers such as baggage handlers have no such advantages. In fact, loading and unloading cargo is probably the most thankless job we have at SAS. It involves crawling into a cramped cargo hold in order to drag out the bags, flinging them into a wagon, driving them to a conveyor belt, and unloading them. The baggage handlers never come into direct contact with the passengers, and so they never get positive or negative feedback from them.

Lacking this, they need clear targets and other means of measuring how well they are meeting their goals. At Arlanda Airport in Stockholm, for example, we have a crack team of baggage handlers. They are fully aware that SAS is aiming for satisfied business customers, and they realize how important it is for the entire SAS operation to be efficient.

We established the general target of having the luggage roll onto the conveyor belt when the passengers arrive at baggage claim. To make this system work, the baggage handlers have to know when they have made their target and when they have not. A system of monitoring results will provide that information. It will also cue their superiors to issue praise or constructive criticism.

Naturally, the system must measure the right indicators. At SAS, we were surprised and embarrassed to discover that our cargo division measured precision only in terms of the amount of cargo and the paperwork attached to it. If the two were separated, we recorded an error. So long as the volume was high and the items stayed together, we recorded a job well done—no matter how many days late the cargo arrived. Though the monitoring system, which measured only turnover, showed that cargo was constantly setting new records, service was clearly not as good as it could have been.

So we asked our cargo people to come up with a new method of measuring. They devised the QualiCargo system, which measured primarily the precision of our service: how quickly did we answer the telephone? Did we meet the promised deadlines? Did the cargo actually arrive with the plane we had booked it on? How long did it take from the time the plane landed until the cargo was ready to be picked up by the customer?

The results of the measurements are published every month. A QualiCargo diagram included in each report compares the various cargo terminals with each other and with their own targets. It graphically shows which station has done the best and which has done the worst. Those stations that achieve their targets are awarded a star and the praise of Mats Mitsell, our operations manager. Those that don't had better be prepared to answer a few questions.

At first we received a lot of criticism for issuing the QualiCargo report. Traditionally Scandinavians refrain from criticizing one another in public. Some people suggested that our employees would not respond well to such criticism. But they have. When we started this system, 80 percent of all shipments arrived at the appointed time. Today we are up to 92 percent.

Are our people working harder than before? No. The SAS cargo staff has always worked with intensity and dedication. But now that a more accurate system of measurement has identified previously unrecognized problems, routines have been changed and resources have been shifted.

For example, the QualiCargo reports indicated that it was taking an unusually long time to deliver cargo to consignees in New York. Having identified the problem, the cargo people in New York hit upon an ingenious solution: they literally knocked down one of the walls in the cargo terminal to create another loading dock. They eliminated the bottleneck, and delivery times improved immediately.

Why hadn't anybody thought of that solution before? Because no one knew the problem existed. Until the QualiCargo report quantified the length of time it took to deliver cargo to consignees, no one was aware that New York was slower than other stations and, thus, probably slower than necessary. For the first time, QualiCargo compared New York with Copenhagen, Stockholm, and other stations worldwide. By measuring the right indicators, we were able to identify a problem area and find a solution that improved service.

The major improvement in precision and speed did not, however, result from visible measures such as these. Rather, it arose from the cargo people's new understanding of what is important to SAS customers. The new strategy and measurements are combined with financial information, so everyone can clearly see the financial consequences of dozens of routine decisions. As a result, people can now focus on the activities that are profitable.

Of course, even before there was a premium on providing delivery as fast as possible. Now the difference is that everyone at SAS cargo knows not only that precision is important but also why (because precision is what the customer pays for), and they know exactly what the components of precision are. It is clear that top priorities are answering telephones, booking shipments, receiving them, forwarding them along with their documentation, receiving at the other end, reconciling cargo and documentation, preparing for customer pick-up, and informing customers when their shipments are ready.

This new insight has had significant effects on the way the cargo division approaches its daily operations. Cargo workers no longer wait for their supervisors to point out things to do. Managers do not need to spend time scheduling coffee breaks and work shifts—everyone knows when there is work to be done and when there is time to relax. Pacing the workload eliminates unnecessary rushing. Most importantly, the employees have renewed energy and commitment—a commitment to doing things right, which is so much easier now that standards and measures for "right" have been set.

# 11

# REWARDING EMPLOYEES

On a December day in 1982, every one of SAS's 20,000 employees received a parcel in the mail. Upon opening it, each found a beautiful gold wristwatch with a second hand in the shape of a tiny airplane. In addition there was a memo outlining new, more liberal regulations governing free trips for employees (an employee benefit at every airline in the world). Also included was a second "little red book," entitled "The Fight of the Century," and an invitation to a party. Finally, there was a letter from me, printed on quality parchment paper, thanking them for the great job they had done during that year in which SAS had vaulted from its worst loss ever to the biggest profit in its history.

The contents of the package may not seem so extraordinary, but the recipients were delighted. Scores of them sent me thank-you letters with messages like: "There I stood, a grown-up, at the post office with my package, and I was so happy that I was ready to cry. It was the first time in all my years at SAS that I had ever received a personal thank-you for what I had done—and, best of all, I felt I deserved it."

Everyone realized, of course, that the letter was pre-printed and that all SAS employees had received identical copies. Nonetheless, they understood that it was meant personally, as evidence that we in top management had appreciated their superb individual efforts.

We had asked 20,000 people to go the extra mile for a year to help pull SAS out of a crisis. Now they deserved our thanks in equal measure. Sooner or later you have to step off the track for a breather. Everyone needs to hear that they have done a good job. It's part of what motivates people and helps them maintain their own self-respect and motivation.

Our "reward" plan had two phases: awarding an individual symbol of recognition, the watch, followed by a joint symbol, the party. The watch was a particularly appropriate gift. Not only was it an expression of our gratitude but it tied in with our successful effort to become the world's most punctual airline.

The second phase was the party. We intended this joint symbol of recognition to underscore the fact that SAS is actually a *group*, albeit a very large one. We held parties all over the world to do it. Four thousand people attended the one in Stockholm alone, including mechanics, pilots, loaders, pursers, air hostesses, secretaries, salesmen, computer technicians, and everyone else, all of whom recognized that we had achieved something collectively—not just individually.

The SAS parties had their predecessors at Linjeflyg. There, much the same story had unfolded: because of the tremendous involvement and enthusiasm of the staff, we were able to transform the company and dramatically improve profits.

The Linjeflyg party should have been easy to organize. Since half of the company's 1,200 employees worked nights and the other half worked days, however, the only time to have a party was when everyone was off work—between midnight and 6:00 A.M. Given that constraint, we flew our staff into the Stockholm airport one evening, held our party in an airplane hangar, and flew them back out early the next morning. A hangar may not seem like a festive location, but all who were there will tell you it was a great party. In fact, it was the first opportunity for everyone at Linjeflyg to meet at the same time.

Though the watches and parties may come once a year, employees work hard on a daily basis, often with little or no recognition. Unfortunately, in many companies the only thing that gets attention is a mistake. Whether you do a good or a poor job—or even if you do nothing at all—no one will bother to comment. It can be disheartening if no one notices when there are slumps or problem-ridden periods. "Does it make any difference if I bungle my job? Doesn't anyone notice it? Why should I exert myself?"

Everyone needs to feel that their contributions are noticed. The work we do and the recognition we get for it contribute to our self-esteem. Especially in a service-oriented business where employees' self-esteem and on-the-job morale have an enormous impact upon customer satisfaction, a word of well-deserved praise can go a long way.

Of course, praise generates energy, but only if it is justified. Receiving unmerited accolades can be an insult that reveals indifference on the part of the bestower. At SAS, for example, we once "thoughtfully" sent thank-you notes to all of the employees who had pitched in to alleviate the effects of a strike. But our effort was not administered carefully, so that even people who had nothing to do with the strike were congratulated. Our good intentions backfired as confusion and resentment ensued.

A company can reinforce its employees' sense of self-worth on a daily basis in a number of ways—even down to their uniforms.

After we decided to focus on the business travel market at SAS, we reassessed our color and design schemes. If we had been concentrating on the tourist trade, we probably would have outfitted the staff in brightly colored, sporty clothing. But as the business traveler's airline, we opted for a more businesslike look, custom designed by Calvin Klein, with conservative styling in dark blue fabric.

Of course, the effort to tailor our company to the business market would have been less than complete if our staff's appearance did not contribute to the image. And since our people spend all their working hours in uniform, they should be given uniforms that they could wear proudly. So we spent $4 million on new uniforms for our 20,000 employees. Like the new carts for the cabin crew and the service-oriented training courses we asked everyone to take, the clothes became a symbol of the new SAS—a way of saying to our frontline people: "We are investing in you because you are important." This message was tangible proof that the new SAS identity affected not just management but was reflected everywhere in the company, including the daily attitude and appearance of each employee.

We ushered in our business look with all the fanfare due the unveiling of a new designer collection. To background music provided by a live band and a prerecorded disco version of "Love Is in the Air," we staged three virtually simultaneous presentations of the entire new corporate identity—at SAS hangars in Oslo, Stockholm, and Copenhagen—attended by our employees, the press, and government officials, including the national ministers of transport.

All of the models were SAS employees, and I even donned a maitre d's white jacket for the grand finale. The affairs were catered with food and drinks for all. And how were they received? With enthusiastic—and sometimes tearful—cheers of approval! By proudly displaying our new look, we communicated to our employees, the media, and the public that we were undergoing an exciting transformation—and that we were here to stay.

For a company that has flattened the pyramid, it becomes particularly important to reinforce the self-worth of individual employees. The old hierarchical structure placed great emphasis on the trappings of power such as offices, titles, and salaries. "Promotion," in hierarchically structured companies, has often meant moving talented people from important jobs to positions of no real substance and increasing their salaries. Many highly competent employees end up merely passing on decisions made by higher-ranking executives.

There is no question that symbols are important. The Chinese army once tried to do away with all visible forms of rank. What arose in place of honorific badges and metals was a hierarchy of chest-pocket pens: the number, color, and size of one's pens indicated one's rank.

I believe an organization that rewards its employees with real job satisfaction and a genuine sense of self-worth is more honest to itself and its staff. A better reward for doing a good job is being awarded well-defined responsibility and trust. Helping talented people blossom and develop is one of management's toughest challenges. Resorting to empty promotions as the way of showing appreciation is tantamount to a confession of failure.

At the same time that we gave the front line new responsibility at SAS, we began working to change attitudes about what was considered a promotion. In a company that has flattened the pyramid, going "up" isn't necessarily an improvement. I wanted people to feel they were being promoted when they received an assignment that gave them an opportunity to accomplish something important, even if it did not come with a fancy title and all the trappings associated with high rank.

I believe a frontline SAS employee ought to be able to describe his job in terms that would make managers and directors in other companies grow pale. "I used to be in charge of twice as many people, but I didn't actually have any influence," he should say. "Sure, I had a big office, but I never saw our staff or customers. Now I am going to be where I'm needed, where I can really do some good."

Simply put, the richest reward of all is being proud of your work. I remember how those I respected frowned when I took my first job at Vingresor just after graduating from the Stockholm School of Economics. One of my most esteemed professors protested that I would be wasting my time on a questionable business. My father was only too happy to remind me that my cousin, who had started working as an accountant for a car dealership, was well on his way toward a respectable, professional position.

Over time, both of these men continued to voice their disapproval of my career choice. My professor informed me regularly of other job openings. My father let it be understood that I was fiddling in a job without a future. Succumbing to their pressure, I applied for a job as a section head at the newly opened Swedish Institute for Informative Labeling, a bleak bureaucracy that didn't fit my style one bit.

Fortunately, I didn't get the job. Back in my office at Vingresor, I grew more and more uncertain about what I wanted. Then one day a customer phoned to ask where a particular tour guide would be working the following season. I told him that the guide was handling bus tours around Lake Boden, on the Swiss-German border.

"Oh, that's too bad," the customer said. "We've already done that trip several times, and we'd like to try something different. You see, 10 years ago, my wife and I went to Egypt, and this fellow was the tour conductor. And, Mr. Carlzon, he gave us the best 14 days of our lives! Since then we always try to pick the trips he leads."

That's when it hit me: if I have a job that allows me to help people have the best weeks of their lives, then no professor in the world can tell me my business is of questionable worth. And my father need not worry about the value of the job, either.

If that man hadn't told me his story, I might have left Vingresor feeling defeated. Instead, he restored my self-esteem and my sense of the value of my job. He also prompted me to reassess my criteria for success in life.

A few years later, I received the greatest reward I've had in my 20 working years.

Vingresor had heavily promoted children's services. "We'll take care of your kids while you go out on the town!" we advertised. To figure out what to do with the kids themselves, we sat down with tour conductors, preschool teachers, and others knowledgeable about children. We took the attitude that children are people with needs, too—and they have their own ideas about what makes a successful holiday.

Knowing how much kids like to have secrets, we organized a club complete with passwords and membership cards. If they couldn't sign their names on the cards, the kids could stamp their thumbprints instead. Special T-shirts and hats would be printed with "Miniclub" in bold letters. The club would even have its own song: "Here Comes the Miniclub."

It was such a great idea we decided the theme of our advertising campaign should be vacations for *children*, not for their parents. So we turned the whole concept around and said: "It's no longer a problem to take Mom and Dad on vacation."

Early one morning on the island of Mallorca, off the eastern coast of Spain, I awoke to the sound of singing somewhere outside. Who would be singing so early in the morning? The voices grew louder, and I peeked through the venetian blinds to see who it was. Then they came into view: 30 deeply tanned Swedish children in T-shirts and hats gleefully marching down the street and singing, "Here Comes the Miniclub"! Believe me, no paycheck or bonus, no plush office or executive perk was ever as wonderful a reward as that!

We *all* need rewards and, further, we work better when we can take pride in the work we're doing. Of course, competent people are paid well for their contributions, but receiving well-defined responsibility and the trust and active interest of others is a much more personally satisfying reward. I believe that by understanding what the employees want from their jobs, what their aims are, and how they want to develop, leaders can heighten their employees' sense of self-worth. And the power behind healthy self-esteem generates the confidence and creativity needed to tackle the new challenges that are constantly around the corner.

# 12

# THE SECOND WAVE

**B**y 1984 it must have seemed to the outside world that SAS had accomplished its goals and could breathe a well-deserved sigh of relief. Passengers were responding positively to our improved service. Our finances had recovered much more quickly than any of us had dared hope. And *Air Transport World* had just named SAS "Airline of the Year." We had achieved everything we had set out to do.

Yet for me, 1984 was a year of agony. I was quickly learning yet another lesson about running a business organization: when you reach your goal, you may become a prisoner of success. As Roald Sokilde, our Danish regional manager, observed, it's tougher to win peace than to win war.

During my first years at SAS, the entire company was unified behind a single, logical goal that everyone could back: "We must become profitable! We cannot be profitable by buying, investing in, and selling aircraft. We have to become profitable by being a service-oriented company that earns its money by being number 1 at service!" That overall goal was clear and unmistakable, and we had a wealth of evidence that it had penetrated everywhere and was accepted by almost everyone. Between 1981 and 1984 all our forces were aligned, and each and every person was striving to surpass his previous best efforts.

But now we had arrived at our objective—before we had given much thought to what we wanted to accomplish next.

The absence of new goals was producing some negative effects at SAS. The atmosphere of togetherness was eroding. The purpose of our work began to be questioned frequently. And our employees' newfound energy began to be redirected toward narrower and more personal objectives. Now that SAS had once again become so profitable, various groups of employees had different ideas about how these profits should be used. One group, for instance, pushed for the purchase of new aircraft. Another decided it was time for SAS to pay its employees higher wages.

Now those interests began to compete against one another. At first it appeared that top management could do little to arrest the deteriorating conditions. We had expressly divested ourselves of the terms of control usually marshaled to bring employees into line. We couldn't issue orders and directives to bring about a renewed buildup of strength. Still worse, we were fully aware that SAS was not completely out of the woods. The immediate crisis had passed, but we had to double profitability to survive over the long run. We needed a new, tangible goal that every individual SAS employee could embrace.

In retrospect I realized that in 1980 we should have set an ultimate, long-term goal and viewed immediate profitability as a short-range subgoal. It would have been much more effective to have told our employees in 1984: "This is where we were in 1980 and this is where we are today. Thank you for all the work you've done to get us here. Now we're going to continue on to our next goal, which is over there."

Instead, we ended up on the defensive.

We came under heavy fire from the pilots, for example, for not buying new planes. "We all thought the wealth of ideas you spouted in 1981 was great and gave the company a new sense of vitality," they said. "But now it looks like the ideas have dried up, and we're left with antiquated aircraft while other companies are buying new planes."

We had obviously failed to communicate to our pilots that we wanted to take the company in an entirely new direction, away from the production-oriented mentality. That's why they didn't understand that one of the most important parts of our strategy was to keep the old planes because they fit the type of service we wanted to sell, better than any new aircraft would.

The misunderstanding was largely my fault. My own statements had fostered resentment among some employees. "We will never buy new aircraft just to give our pilots new cockpits to sit in," I had said in 1981. "We will never buy new aircraft just to give our mechanics something new to fiddle with. We'll only buy new aircraft when it enhances our value to our business travelers and in that way makes us more competitive."

This was my way of explaining that we were now a market-oriented company focused on competitiveness, not technology. But the pilots and mechanics interpreted it otherwise, and in retrospect it is easy to see why.

"Does he think we want new planes just to play with?" the pilots asked among themselves. "Is it only passengers whose desires count?" Similarly, the mechanics asked, "Did he say we *fiddle* with airplanes? Doesn't he realize that we are professionals?"

Of course, these employees had harbored their concerns all along. But in the initial rush to success they had set them aside. Now, with the goal achieved and people looking for new ways to release their energy, problems such as these resurfaced and created a confidence gap between management and the employees.

One example was the debate that broke out about "safety," a highly emotional issue. When we made the transition from a production-oriented to a market-oriented company in 1981, we had pushed the service orientation so vigorously that we lost our footing a bit on the technical and operational side. I point a finger at myself alone for this shortcoming.

I made the unforgivable mistake of assuming. I assumed that everybody understood that safety and technical quality were a given, someting that could never be questioned. When I talked about service I meant the *total* service, what the customer pays for and gets, in which the primary ingredient is safety.

But many employees misunderstood. They saw service as being what you get across the check-in counter or onboard. We never intended for our pilots or mechanics to put punctuality, for example, before safety.

The controversy started within the company but was fueled from the outside when prominent Swedish newspapers received untold phone calls from dissatisfied SAS workers eager to "divulge" safety shortcomings.

Finding ourselves on the defensive, we in management established safety committees. We hired foreign consultants to examine the entire operation and report how we compared internationally. We even met with the most blatantly aggressive newspapers in order to vindicate our excellent safety record. To outsiders our staunch defense must have smacked of an indirect admission that something wasn't right. In truth, our flight safety was never jeopardized. Together with the Australians, the Scandinavians have the best flight safety records in the world. Now that the misinterpretation has been corrected, we have achieved the proper balance between an aggressive commercial operation on the one hand and technical/operational excellence on the other.

Soon afterward other staff members presented new wage demands. The Swedish cabin crews felt shortchanged compared to their colleagues in the other Scandinavian countries. The personnel at Scandinavian stations pressed for a review of the entire wage and salary system.

Again, management started retreating.

By now, every time we met with large groups of personnel, the sessions ended with presentations of demands for more free trips, improved coordination of meal times for cabin crews, a revamped vacation planning system, and so on. To each point we simply responded, "Certainly, we'll do that" or "We'll look into that." But we knew that we weren't making real progress in satisfying what became an endless list of demands.

After one of these meetings, one of my closest friends and colleagues approached me saying, "Jan, this can't go on any longer. Now we have to begin making demands again."

Of course, I realized. That was it! Caught up in our efforts to maintain the excellent spirit we had built at SAS, we retreated from the ultimatums being fired at us rather than countering with some of our own.

By establishing our original goal, we had placed a demand on our employees. But now that there was no goal, a kind of reversal had set in. We had unleashed new energy, new motivation; with the goal achieved and the motivation still there, people then began setting their own individual goals, scattering in all directions and making different demands of the company. It was a graphic illustration of the need for top management to direct all forces toward a common goal.

At the next big staff meeting, we were again swamped with demands. This time I suggested, "Let's make a list of your problems with SAS."

The list grew to the same old complaints. "So you are happy with the rest?" I asked. "That's great. That means 95 percent of everything at SAS is fine. Now we will take care of the remaining 5 percent, which we promise we will fix within a given deadline. Those people in charge of solving each problem will make progress reports to you, not to me."

Then I went on to something new. "Now that we've addressed the specific problems you aired, I want you to know that we, in turn, are going to make some specific demands of you." And I voiced our expectations of the company in general and of frontline personnel in particular: provide more service at less cost and cut expenses that don't result in more revenue. Above all, we reaffirmed our commitment to being the businessman's airline. Admittedly, these "demands" were not new—they constituted the essence of our customer-driven company—but I pointedly reminded our employees of our primary responsibility: to serve the paying customers.

I really don't know what reaction I had expected, but what I got was applause. Afterward, at least 10 people told me virtually the same thing: "You really woke us up! We are actually in good shape here, and of course it's up to us to pitch in and help. As long as you take care of our needs, then you're going to see some sparks fly!"

At last, we had returned to the offensive, and the effect on employee morale was immediate. Part of it, of course, was psychological. Everyone wants a challenge. When we promised to fulfill the employees' requests and challenged them to rise to a new level of service, mutual respect was restored.

But the job was not completed. We still needed a new overall goal that would allow us to concentrate all our forces in one direction again.

I had racked my brain for an objective that would engage everyone at SAS. I had asked everyone I encountered in the company: "Is there anything that will grab the interest of every SAS employee? What do people think about while they're on the job? What worries them? Where do we face a common threat?"

One concern was voiced again and again. For years, SAS and the other European airlines had operated in a highly regulated environment that protected us from the cut-throat competition we had seen develop in the United States after its airline industry was deregulated. But what if deregulation came to Europe? What would happen to our cozy market niche if suddenly our competitors were allowed to go after our customers virtually unrestrained?

Here was a tangible threat that could affect every SAS employee. Could we transform it into a positive, new objective around which to unite the company's resources?

I recalled what had happened when the U.S. banking industry was deregulated. A single company had seen what was coming. Every month for five years, the management had summoned different staff members and asked: "What would the consequences be if we were faced with free competition? What would happen in your area? What new conditions would affect you?" On the day deregulation became law, this company was prepared. It knew where the new opportunities were, grabbed hold of them, and immediately took an enormous lead over its shortsighted competitors.

I personally had observed the same chain of events in the American airline business. The two companies best prepared for deregulation were American Airlines and United Airlines. For those airlines that hadn't anticipated it, deregulation became a competitive hell. For these two, it was more like a fresh opportunity. Today the two are by far the leading airlines in the United States and among the most profitable in the world.

Maybe preparing for freer competition could be the core of a new strategy at SAS. Could we capitalize on the concern that already existed in the company? Could we formulate an objective that would counter this unrest constructively? Could we establish a goal of developing our company not just to survive in a world of free competition but to expand and excel in such a world?

It felt as if we had struck the right chord immediately. We hadn't invented a goal. Rather, we had developed one out of a concern that had been there all along.

Having identified our goal, we moved on to designing new strategies. First we studied the effects of U.S. deregulation. The new business environment inevitably puts a squeeze on revenue. Competitors lower their prices; new entrants appear on the scene. Companies must fight to maintain their positions, and revenue no longer flows automatically.

It is no coincidence that U.S. airlines are more efficient today than they were in a regulated environment (they have reduced their costs by roughly 25 percent). Neither is it a coincidence that they are more efficient than we Europeans are. To survive in a business environment where market share and revenue are no longer givens, a company must be able to reduce its costs.

If we centered our new campaign only around increased efficiency, however, we might wind up with the same result we faced in 1984. Perhaps it would work for a year, but concerns would once again arise about matters such as safety or technical standards. At worst, an overzealous efficiency campaign could hurt the quality of service, and that would be fatal. Having established a vital and profitable organization based on high-quality service to business customers, we couldn't afford to destroy it in the name of efficiency. We also couldn't leave ourselves open to the charge that we were sacrificing safety. Efficiency had to be part of a larger strategy. But what?

At this point, we turned to SAS's impressive history of meeting the challenges of the times. When the commercial airline industry was growing in the 1950s, SAS was at the leading edge of operative developments—important advances in navigation, improved techniques for flying in bad weather, increased safety during takeoff and landing, pioneering shortcuts through polar routes, and so on. All were driving forces behind the business.

During the 1960s and '70s, SAS was at the forefront of technical developments of the aircraft themselves, which, during those decades, was the most important advance. SAS was the first airline to buy and fly the Caravelle, the French-built jetliner with twin engines in the tail, and was active in developing the DC-9, which became our workhorse airplane.

The 1980s, of course, ushered in a new market situation with a greater emphasis on competition. This time the technology itself became secondary to the focus on service and customer orientation. We came out on top once again and were named "Airline of the Year" for 1983.

In other words, every decade had had its own characteristic competitive situation, and SAS had unfailingly taken the lead in each. Building for the future had to involve not only increased efficiency for the short term but also a reinforcement of all three areas—operations, aircraft, and service—that had made us a great airline in the past.

So we decided on this strategy: SAS would work efficiently and skillfully to survive in a free-market situation.

We would remain committed to unwavering quality in the vital areas of operations, aircraft, and service. Upon this firm foundation we would mount a determined drive to boost efficiency and hence stride with confidence into a competitive deregulated market.

How does this translate into concrete terms? Our overall strategy of catering to the business traveler will not change. In addition to sustaining that goal, we will tackle three new areas of development.

First, in an era of free competition, we must become at least 25 percent more efficient, as the successful American airlines have done. We will not achieve this goal through across-the-board cost-cutting. Instead, we will approach costs as we did in 1981—as a resource for improving our overall profitability. By cutting some costs and using others more effectively to increase revenue, we hope to "do more with less."

Second, we need to set up a system of communication, information, and reservations that will give us a firm grip on our entire market. United and American have already established their own reservation and information systems, partly to maintain their current leading positions and partly to penetrate new markets, including those in which SAS is now strong. We must follow suit or be forced to purchase our reservations and information services from an outside source—maybe even from a competitor like United or American.

Third, we must develop a more competitive system of routes, flight frequencies, and departure times. In part, this will entail adopting the hub-and-spoke example of U.S. airlines. And that, in turn, will require giving greater attention to Copenhagen Airport. Copenhagen is our gateway airport, our counterpart to London, Paris, or Frankfurt. People have long considered Copenhagen Airport less attractive than the others, but we must change their perception if we are to prosper. To that end, SAS and Danish authorities have budgeted $800 million for renovations and expansion.

The ultimate goal: by 1990 SAS will be the most efficient airline in Europe.We will have a competitive, world-wide network of routes. We will be market leader s in service, quality, and safety. We will be able to compete profitably on all distances and with all sizes of planes. By then, we will have the financial strength we need to modernize our fleet, and a "Three-P Plane" will probably be a reality. We will have turned the threat of possible deregulation into an opportunity to secure an even more formidable market position.

We call this "the second wave" at SAS. It differs from the first wave in one crucial respect: we are trying to be more patient. The first time, we hot-wired the entire system and went straight to the front lines and the market to sell the strategies. On the brink of disaster, we had no alternative. Now we have a little more time to present our plan and ensure that each of our employees accepts it and fully understands its implications for their individual responsibilities.

The early evidence tells us that we are still on the right strategic course. The Danish business paper, *Boersen*, ranked us first for having the best corporate image. Also, *Air Transport World* announced that they selected SAS's passenger service as the best for 1986.Wanting to share this prize with our employees—they're the ones who really earned it—we distributed to all 30,000 a solid gold heart. It is a small but tangible symbol that each individual is at the heart of our success.

Some people seem to think that SAS's future depends on whether we buy Boeing 737s instead of DC-9s or IBM computer equipment instead of Hewlett Packard. But ultimately SAS's future depends on people. Our continued success requires the full support of our traditionally high standards on the part of all our staff members and their willingness to strive toward our efficiency targets. That's why we're investing $10 million to inform and train all SAS staff members through a program of study circles, groups, and discussions.

Many people were quick to opine that free competition will never hit the European airline industry. "You are crying 'wolf'," they accused me, "and that is tantamount to manipulating your employees."

To them I say: If the competition stays at about the same level as it is today, then we can handle it without having to do anything special. But if we improve our efficiency, then we'll be even stronger in the future.

If competition is opened a limited amount and we haven't prepared ourselves, we could be in trouble. But if we take steps now, then we won't have to play a risky game of catch-up.

If competition is completely opened up, we'll certainly run into problems if we're caught unawares. We'll be faced with crises, panic, cutbacks, layoffs, and possibly worse. However, if we are prepared, the chances are good that we will fare very well.

What's more, if SAS is more efficient than any other carrier could be, then there will actually be no reason for government authorities to open up the market.

Sure, no one knows whether we'll ever really face free competition. But the conclusion is very simple: if we prepare ourselves today for tough competition tomorrow, we have everything to gain. We need never rely strictly on good fortune. Whatever the circumstance, we will be in control of our own future.

Although some people have criticized our passion for goal-setting as bordering on the hysterical, I disagree. Larger goals help us see beyond our daily tasks. People want challenges in their jobs and lives. By setting goals as we have at SAS, we can contribute to our employees' well-being and, together, we can strive to serve our customers better and better.

I make no claim to having discovered a unique approach to doing business. Certainly, leaders at many other companies appreciate the importance of ascertaining the business climate and aligning the company's goals, strategy, and organizational structure with it. They, too, set ambitious objectives and talk about decentralization as a means of achieving them.

In fact, many believe that they already have decentralized their organizations and tell their employees, "You can make independent decisions now." But I challenge these leaders as to whether they're passing real responsibility and authority on to their employees. Until they do, and until they choose and communicate a goal that *every* employee can rally around, the leader never truly divests himself of central control and the employees always need the boss to intervene on matters large and small. They can't be sure what is right or wrong because they are not privy to the goal or the strategies for reaching it. Delegating without giving people the prerequisites for independent decision-making leads nowhere.

Empowering employees with real responsibility and authority requires a radically different organizational structure. The model is horizontal, and the work roles are redefined.

The first level is responsible for guiding the company into the future, anticipating threats to current business, and scanning for new opportunities. People at this level establish goals and develop strategies for reaching them. Of course, this entails making decisions, but not regarding specific actions.

The next level is responsible for planning and allocating the available resources by investing money or recruiting people—in other words, doing everything necessary to enable the people at the operative level to carry out the strategies that top management has established. Again, these are not decisions on specific actions. Rather, they are a means of creating the prerequisites for others to make those decisions.

The third level is what I call the front line, or operations. This is where all the specific decisions should be made—all decisions necessary to run the company in accordance with top management's goals and strategies.

You might think that the views I've presented here are familiar and obvious. Why is it so easy to talk about decentralization? Because it's such a logical line of reasoning. Only the customer, and the customer alone, will pay our costs and provide our profits. So, we have to conduct all business planning from the customer's point of view. Who knows best what the customer wants? Of course, those who work out in the front lines, closest to the market. Consequently, it is those people who should have maximum influence on how we shape our products, and the greatest amount of responsibility and authority should be pushed their way.

Many agree that this philosophy contains tremendous potential, so why do so few actually try to implement it? In truth, it is a very ambitious and sometimes elusive approach that conflicts with the ingrained views of work roles. It requires extraordinary patience, perseverance, and courage to see it through. Fortunately, the front line and the market itself are reliable guides for remaining on track.

At SAS we have been working very diligently at flattening our pyramids and remaining true to our goals. The results—far more than just financial—have been fantastic, and we continue to prepare for an even better future.

The executive who shares my views on human resources will realize that he must give all of his employees an opportunity to understand the company's guiding vision. Only then can they really pitch in and give all they've got. Only then can each and every one assume full responsibility for his own share of the overall goal. Only then can you unleash the mighty energy generated by a group of enthusiastic people.

There is no better way to sum up my experience than with the story about the two stone cutters who were chipping square blocks out of granite. A visitor to the quarry asked what they were doing.

The first stone cutter, looking rather sour, grumbled, "I'm cutting this damned stone into a block."

The second, who looked pleased with his work, replied proudly, "I'm on this team that's building a cathedral."

A worker who can envision the whole cathedral and who has been given responsibility for constructing his own portion of it is far more satisfied and productive than the worker who sees only the granite before him. A true leader is one who designs the cathedral and then shares the vision that inspires others to build it.

# ABOUT THE AUTHOR

**Jan Carlzon** was born in Nykoping, Sweden, in 1941. After receiving his M.B.A. from the Stockholm School of Economics in 1967, he joined Vingresor, Sweden's largest tour operator, first as product manager and later as head of marketing. In 1974, when the package-tour business was in a tailspin because of the first energy crisis, he was named managing director of Vingresor at the age of 32 and soon reversed that company's economic decline. In 1978 he became managing director of Linjeflyg, Sweden's major domestic airline, and in 1981 he took command as president and chief executive officer of SAS, the consortium of the national airlines of Denmark, Norway, and Sweden. At both Linjeflyg and SAS his leadership turned heavy economic losses into healthy profits within a year. Mr. Carlzon is frequently invited to give talks and interviews worldwide on leadership and customer-oriented business strategies.

# There's an epidemic with 27 million victims. And no visible symptoms.

It's an epidemic of people who can't read.

Believe it or not, 27 million Americans are functionally illiterate, about one adult in five.

The solution to this problem is you... when you join the fight against illiteracy. So call the Coalition for Literacy at toll-free **1-800-228-8813** and volunteer.

**Volunteer
Against Illiteracy.
The only degree you need
is a degree of caring.**

Ad Council  Coalition for Literacy